Foremothers

Janice Nunnally-Cox

FOREMOTHERS

WOMEN OF THE BIBLE

The Seabury Press · New York

ACKNOWLEDGMENTS

I wish to thank many people.

For my husband, Geoffrey Price: for his enthusiasm and encouragement and bedrock belief in me. He brought light to many a dark day.

For my parents, Harriet Nunnally Cox and Alvon Richards Cox: for all the love and hope they have given me.

For my own foremothers: Rose Pugin Nunnally, Catherine Mulvahill Pugin, Laila Richards Cox, and especially Alice Lewis–Richards: poet, suffragette, temperance leader, author.

For my early teachers: Ellen Campbell, and Richard Snyder, and Bob Bronson.

For the good people of the Church of the Epiphany, Washington.

For my sister priests: Carole Crumley, Gwyneth Bohr, Catherine Powell, Lee McGee; and for Ruth Libbey.

For my many women friends who are like shining sun, especially: Judy Hanson, Pinky Dalton, Nan Simpson, Joan Hickey, Carol Dietsch, Darlene Wright Van Dyke, Octavia Seawill.

And for Bronwyn and Caitlin.

Second printing

1981
The Seabury Press
815 Second Avenue
New York, N.Y. 10017

Library of Congress Cataloging in Publication Data

Nunnally-Cox, Janice.
Foremothers : women of the Bible.

1. Women in the Bible. I. Title.
BS575.N86 220.9′2 81-5675
ISBN 0-8164-2329-6 (pbk.) AACR2

For my mother, Harriet.

CONTENTS

PREFACE

For the past several years I have traveled around the Washington, D.C. area, giving a series of talks on biblical women. People always seem quite interested in the introductory material, that is, the stories and beginnings that precede the writing of a book. I offer this in part to you now, so that you may see with my eyes and hear a bit with my ears, and, finally, sense a direction home. For these stories are, in a way, like going home. It is difficult to know which way home lies until we have seen with certainty where we began, where we have come from, and where we are going.

The title, *Foremothers*, has seemed to cause no small stir. When people ask, What is the title of your book? and I reply, *Foremothers*, there is an inevitable silence. Then another pause, and: Oh. You mean four mothers. Now let's see; who were those mothers? Mary, Elizabeth . . . . Or: For mothers? Why is it just for mothers? What about fathers? And more confusion. Even when I spell it, people often fail to understand. Only when I add: *foremothers*, as in *forefathers*, do people really understand. This in itself seems a bit startling. The second surprising thing often occurs in a class situation when people finally do understand the title. There follows a corporate chuckle: Ah! Oh yes! *Foremothers*—how clever. It has not been my intention that the title be clever or funny; rather, I would hope it a word we recognize when we hear it. A useful word, a practical word, an everyday ordinary word: *foremothers*; standing by itself, understood.

A few stories also travel with this series: When I was in seminary I offered an outline of *Foremothers* in lieu of a required paper. The professor, a priest, said he supposed it would be acceptable as long as it wasn't prejudiced. My response was: but that is the whole point. Another time I gave the series in a parish where none of the priests (male) was ever in attendance. One did stop by briefly during a particularly exciting class. Some time later he met my husband and, on finding we were married, commented: Oh yes, fascinating girl, your wife; but terribly prejudiced. My husband replied that I was working with rather biased material. And finally, on the eve before I was to begin the series in a parish, one of the priests (male) questioned me on what I was about to do: now what is this thing? he said; something about women? I named the title, we moved through that confusion, and then he said: mmmm. biblical women; well now, there's Gomer . . . . He could not recall any more. These stories are funny and sad and, I hope, soon to be no more.

Concerning beginnings, this series began in 1975 when I saw a sheet entitled "Giants of the Old Testament." A Christian education director passed this to her children for study. Only the men of Israel were listed, except for one woman, Ruth, a Moabite at that, and an acceptably obedient woman. I had already graduated from seminary, but was somewhat unsettled to discover that I could name only a handful of biblical women. Aren't there any more? I asked myself. Who were they? What did they do? And so I began. Literature and references concerning these women were few and far between—quite hard soil for digging.

Eventually, over the years, various purposes began to unfold. At the first I simply wished to name the women, bring them to surface. But during the process of the naming other things occurred: I began to notice blatant and subtle prejudices on the writers' parts, against the women. At first it amused me; then it didn't. A second purpose, then, was to uncover the bias, bring it to light. And, for a third purpose, I am now trying to see the history: move beyond and behind and away from the biblical stories themselves; move back to the Goddess of 25,000 B.C., move forward to women priests of 2,000 A.D.—see the movement, the suppression, the abiding strength.

So we always come back, full circle, to woman: *ishshah*. We have all come a very long way, and the biblical women, too, have stories to tell. Their stories speak of hope, suffering, dreams, despair, and mostly of endurance. They are magnificient women. Nothing can take them from our books or from our hearts; nothing, no one, can imitate their wit, their strength, their humor, or their power. For they are, above all else, filled with power: *chutzpah*, visible for all to see. May you enjoy them as I have and do, and may the God of Sarah, Rebekah, and Rachel continue with you on the long journey home.

Janice Ellen Nunnally-Cox
Arlington, Virginia
September 1980

INTRODUCTION

> In the beginning God created the heavens and the earth. The earth was without form and void, and darkness was upon the face of the deep; and the Spirit of God was moving over the face of the waters. (Genesis 1:1,2)

Genesis contains two creation stories, one known as the Priestly story of creation, the other as the Yahwist story of creation. They both tell us that God created all things: light, darkness, firmament, dry land, seas, plants, fruit trees, sun, moon, stars, birds, sea monsters, cattle, creeping things, beasts, and people. The content of the two stories is similar, but the order of creation, quite dissimilar. For woman, this order of things has made a great deal of difference over the centuries.

The Priestly account of creation appears in Genesis 1:1–2:4a; it is the later of the two stories, dated approximately 450 BC.[1] The writer tells us of all the wonderful creations of God beginning with light, moving through earth, seas, sky, plants, animals, and ending with human beings:

> Then God said, "Let us make man in our image, after our likeness. . . ." So God created man in his own image, in the image of God he created him; male and female he created them. And God blessed them. . . . (Genesis 1:26a, 27, 28a)

In the order of things, human beings come last and they come together. Female and male they appear, formed in the holy likeness of God, and blessed by God. As far as we can tell, neither creature is subordinate to the other: both are formed at once, both have authority over the earth, both are in God's favor. God creates man, *'adham,* meaning humankind,[2] and God sees that it is very good. After this God rests, weary from work, and pleased with creation.

The Yawhist account holds quite a different tone. This is a much earlier story, written approximately 950 BC,[3] and appearing in Genesis 2:4b–3:24. In this account creation forms very differently: we hear first of man (*'adham*), then of trees, beasts, and birds, then lastly of woman:

> So the Lord God caused a deep sleep to fall upon the man, and while he slept took one of his ribs and closed up its place with flesh; and the rib which the Lord God had taken from the man he made into a woman and brought her to the man.
>
> Genesis 2:21, 22)

The story then names the female *ishshah,* Woman, and the male *ish,* Man. We then hear that the man and woman are naked and not ashamed.

Following this comes the familiar serpent story: the serpent, a subtle creature, beguiles the woman, and she eats forbidden fruit. She gives fruit to her husband, who also eats; they see their nakedness, and are ashamed. The Lord God, angry at their transgression, sentences the woman to increased pain in childbearing and the rule of her husband; the man is told he shall toil all the days of his life. You are dust, says God, and to dust you shall return. God then drives the woman and the man, now called Eve and Adam, out of the garden of Eden.

The contrast between the two stories is striking. In the one, woman is equal to man; in the other, she is subordinate. In the Priestly account creation is simultaneous; in the Yahwist version woman comes decidedly after man, even though the term for 'man' is again *'adham,* or humankind. In the first story God blesses the people, calls them good, and then takes time to rest. The second story is filled with fear, anger, and strife: God takes no holy time of rest, and the people are not called good.

The stories present us with a choice: it is for us to decide which story holds high meaning. Can we really believe the old serpent tale? Would God really have been so harsh? Could the woman, really, have been the origin of so much discontent? Many of the writers throughout history apparently think so. And many of the stories we are about to hear are told through the eyes and hearts of those who truly believe woman to be subordinate to man. She is somehow less: less strong, less intelligent, less wise, less good. But fortunately for us the stories of the Bible hold their own power, their own strength, most times in spite of the writers' bias.

So we shall move through the many stories, seeing here and there where the Genesis rib narrative reflects, and where the Priestly story influences. The burden of the reading may become heavy; the shame and sorrow and outrage a bit too much to bear. But keep in mind the power, too, and the strength and regality of woman. For she is indeed royal, bearing proud her many lives. And most of all, take heart: for we see Jesus, and in him the clear light shines. We see him touch and heal and call and name woman, and raise her to himself: to his power, his authority, his compassion, his wisdom. The bonds are broken: shattered, loosed, forever free.

As one biblical writer says: Do not be weary in well-doing. And do not lose hope. For we are called to hold to the vision of creation: formed by God, in the image of God, with the likeness of God. And it is good: it is very good.

·I·

WOMAN AND ISRAEL

ONE

Matriarchs

1. "Princess" and "mother of nations"; woman who laughs when God says she will have a child in old age. Wife of Abraham. **2.** Egyptian maid and servant of Sarai. Bears Abraham a son; calls him Ishmael. **3.** Two young sisters of Sodom who seduce their father in a cave, and bear him children. **4.** Daughter of Bethuel, fair maiden at the well. Marries Isaac and bears twins, Esau and Jacob. **5.** Older, less favored daughter of Laban; marries Jacob through her father's trickery. Bears several sons and a daughter. **6.** Younger, beautiful daughter of Laban. Marries Jacob and bears two sons, Joseph and Benoi. Steals her father's household gods. **7.** Only daughter of Leah. Raped by Shechem, a Hivite prince; is avenged by her brothers. **8.** Woman who is denied motherhood rights by father-in-law Judah; seduces him by roadside and is sentenced to die.

In regard to marriage, divorce, and penalties for adultery, it is difficult to escape the conclusion that the subordination of woman as in the rib narrative of creation (Genesis 2:7–25) prevailed over the equality of "male and female" implied in the Priestly narrative of Genesis 1:27-30.[1]

A woman of Israel was considered, for the most part, property. The Decalogue or "ten words" of Exodus 20 lists the wife among a neighbor's possessions, not to be coveted. In marriage the woman, or more likely young girl, passed from the rule of her father to the rule of her husband. Parents arranged the marriages, often at an early age, and the child had little or no choice in the matter. The father received a "bride price" for his daughter, according to the Law. Exodus indirectly mentions this marriage present:

> If a man seduces a virgin who is not betrothed, and lies with her, he shall give the marriage present for her, and make her his wife. If her father utterly refuses to give her to him, he shall pay money equivalent to the marriage present for virgins.
> (Exodus 22:16, 17)

The woman, for her part, was expected to have an acceptable dowry, and with this the bargain was closed. Once married, the woman faced other matters: often she was not the only wife, as polygamy was common. She, however, had no other husbands. She was expected to produce offspring, namely sons, and if she did not, her position was much less honorable. Daughters were of little account; indeed, a woman was rendered doubly unclean for birthing a girl:

> If a woman conceives, and bears a male child, then she shall be unclean seven days; as at the time of her menstruation. . . . But if she bears a female child, then she shall be unclean two weeks. . . .
> (Leviticus 12:2,5)

Further, if a woman's husband died, or if she was "put away," she came under the protection of a grown son or her own family. Levirate marriage, ancient widespread custom where the brother-in-law would marry his deceased brother's wife, could be rejected by the man, but not the woman.[2]

Concerning divorce and adultery, a woman had little recourse. A husband could divorce his wife for "some indecency," and send her away:

> When a man takes a wife and marries her, if then she finds no favor in his eyes because he has found some indecency in her, and he writes her a bill of divorce and puts it in her hand and sends her out of his house. . . . (Deuteronomy 24:1)

The passage concludes by saying the former wife cannot return to the husband once she remarries and again is divorced, for she will be defiled. Adultery was considered a crime against the husband's rights, so both adulterer and adulteress were stoned to death.[3] In some more ancient accounts, however, the involved woman was punished by death, while the man was not.

Other inequities abound: Women had no property rights, except in rare instances when there were no sons, and even then there were family restrictions; a woman's oath could be easily disavowed by her father or husband, whereas a man's was immutable; a male Hebrew slave was freed after six years of service, but a woman was kept by her master for his son or the master himself.

Despite these limitations, the picture was not entirely bleak. For within the family structure woman could indeed be a powerful figure: a matriarch of respect and influence. She maintained her wit, her charm, her humor, her strength, her intellect, her position. Her power lay not in family rights or privileges, but in her wisdom and perseverance; her accumulated survival instincts. She was a striking figure: suppressed but somehow dominant, somehow influential, and her subordination made her oddly strong.

To these women we now turn: to the matriarchs in a patriarchal society, to the ancient stories of the book of Genesis. These are the greatest of the many wondrous tales of Israel.

Sarah and Hagar

> And Abram and Nahor took wives; the name of Abram's wife was Sarai . . . . Now Sarai was barren; she had no child.
> (Genesis 11:29, 30)

> She had an Egyptian maid whose name was Hagar; and Sarai said to Abram, "Behold now, the Lord has prevented me from bearing children; go into my maid; it may be that I shall obtain children by her." (Genesis 16:1,2)

The first mention of Sarai describes her as barren. Sarai and Abram are living, with their larger family, in the land of Haran. God calls Abraham to leave his ancestral home and go to a new country. There, God says, "I will make of you a great nation, and I will bless you. . . ." So Abraham goes, and Lot, his brother's son, goes with him, along with Sarai and all their many possessions. They travel to the land of Canaan, where Abram builds an altar to the Lord. During a later time of famine, the family continues on to Egypt in search of food.

Upon arrival in Egypt, Abram pleads with Sarai: I know you are a woman beautiful to behold, he says; the Egyptians will kill me, thinking you are my wife. Say you are my sister, that it may go well with me. Sarai does so, and when the princes of the Pharaoh see her, she is taken into Pharaoh's house. Abram, in return, receives abundantly: sheep, oxen, asses, menservants, maidservants, and camels. But the ruse does not last long. The Lord afflicts Pharaoh's house with great plagues, and Abram confesses. Pharaoh orders Abram to take Sarai and be gone, and the family begins the long trek back to Canaan.

Sometime later we hear of Sarai's barrenness once again. Sarai gives Abram her Egyptian maid, Hagar, in hopes that she will bear a son. Abram "hearkens to the voice of Sarai," and Hagar conceives. Hagar, says the story, now looks with contempt on her mistress.

> And Sarai said to Abram, "May the wrong done to me be on you! I gave my maid to your embrace, and when she saw that she had conceived, she looked on me with contempt. May the Lord judge between you and me!" (Genesis 16:5)

Abram replies that Hagar is in Sarai's power; she can do as she pleases with her. Sarai then deals harshly with Hagar, and Hagar flees to the wilderness. There she meets an angel who promises her a son. You shall call his name Ishmael, he says, and he shall be a wild ass of a man. Hagar indeed bears Abram a son, and Abram calls him Ishmael.

When Abram is ninety-six years old, God changes his name. "No longer shall your name be Abram, but your name shall be Abraham, for I have made you the father of a multitude of nations." God also makes a covenant with Abraham, a covenant of circumcision. Every male in Abraham's family is to be circumcised, and all the descendants following. If you do this, says God, the land of Canaan will be yours forever. God further changes Sarai's name to Sarah, for she is to be princess of her people, mother of nations, and she shall bear a son.

Upon hearing the news of a son, Abraham falls on his face and laughs:

> Shall a child be born to a man who is a hundred years old? Shall Sarah, who is ninety years old, bear a child? And Abraham said to God, "O that Ishmael might live in thy sight!"
>
> (Genesis 17:17, 18)

God corrects Abraham: Sarah will bear a son, God says, and you will call his name Isaac. God and Abraham talk on, and Abraham returns home to circumcise all the males of his household.

The Lord next appears to Abraham by the oaks of Mamre. Abraham sits at the door of his tent in the heat of the day. Three men, elsewhere called angels, appear in front of him, and Abraham bows to the earth. He entreats the strangers to rest under a tree and take water and bread with him. They agree, and Abraham runs to Sarah, asking her for meal cakes, and to a servant, who prepares a calf. Then Abraham returns to the men. Where is Sarah your wife? they ask. In the tent, replies Abraham. The narrative swiftly changes to "the Lord," who says Sarah will have a son, come spring. In the meantime, Sarah has her ear to the tent door. The story describes Sarah and Abraham as being old, "advanced in age," and it has ceased to be with Sarah "after the manner of women." Sarah begins to chuckle to herself, thinking no one will hear: "After I have grown old, and my husband is old, shall I have pleasure?" The Lord then questions Abraham:

> Why did Sarah laugh and say, "Shall I indeed bear a child, now that I am old?" Is anything too hard for the Lord?
>
> (Genesis 18:13, 14)

Sarah denies her laughter, for she is afraid. God responds with: No, but you did laugh.

The next we hear of Sarah and Abraham, they are journeying once again, this time to the land of Gerar, where Abimelech is king. Once again Abraham says of Sarah: she is my sister. Abimelech takes Sarah, but God comes to him in a dream. You are a dead man, says God, for this is another man's wife. Abimelech pleads innocence and integrity, and God excuses him. Abimelech goes at once to find Abraham: Why did you do this thing? he asks. Because I thought there is no fear of God here, says Abraham, and they will kill me because of Sarah. Besides, he adds:

> . . .she is indeed my sister, the daughter of my father but not the daughter of my mother; and she became my wife.
>
> (Genesis 20:12)

The king gives Abraham gifts of sheep, oxen, slaves, and silver, and also returns Sarah. Abraham prays to God and the wombs of the house of Abimelech are opened: God rewards them with many new children.

It is now spring, and Sarah gives birth to a boy-child. Abraham calls him Isaac, meaning "he laughs." The child grows and Abraham holds a great feast for him. But Sarah sees Ishmael, son of Hagar, at play with her son Isaac. She says to Abraham:

> Cast out this slave woman with her son; for the son of this slave woman shall not be heir with my son Isaac. (Genesis 21:10)

Abraham is not pleased, but God tells him to do whatever Sarah tells him, for "through Isaac shall your descendants be named." So Abraham rises early in the morning, gives Hagar bread and a skin of water, and sends her away with her child to wander in the wilderness of Beer-sheba. God protects Hagar and Ishmael, and they live their days in the wilderness of Paran.

We last hear of Sarah at Hebron, in the land of Canaan. She is now very old, one hundred twenty-seven years, and here she dies. Abraham mourns for Sarah, and weeps. He goes to the Hittites, saying he is a stranger, and asks for property that he might bury his dead. The Hittites call him "mighty prince" and give him choice of the finest sepulchres: Abraham buys the cave of Machpelah, in a field, and then he buries Sarah.

Several things are readily apparent in the story of Sarah and Abraham. First, she holds powerful sway over Abraham. It is he who asks her permission to call her sister, however questionable his actions may be. In the instance of Hagar, Sarah is the one who suggests the liason, and Abraham does her bidding. After Hagar conceives and Sarah shouts at Abraham, he merely humors her. And when Sarah later insists that Hagar and Ishmael be cast out, Abraham once again complies with her wishes, even though it means losing a son and an heir.

God, also, seems to be on Sarah's side at times. God defends Sarah three times: once with plagues against Pharoah, once by opening the closed wombs of Abimelech's house, and third by siding with Sarah over the Ishmael incident. If we were true to scholarship and intent, we cannot surmise that these are actually acts of God, but rather the writer's view of events and occurrences, as he later interprets them. It is to the writer's credit that he would interpret the happenings to a woman's influence. We can, however, understand that the writer needs to preserve Sarah at all cost, for she is to bear Abraham's heir, and herein lies her worth.

One incident, however, clearly contradicts God's defense of Sarah. The story of Sarah laughing at the tent door is in stark contrast to the covenant talk between God and Abraham. For when Abraham laughs at the announcement of a son, when he further rolls on the ground in mirth, nothing happens. God ignores the outbreak and continues conversation. When Sarah chuckles over the thought of having a son, and that behind a tent flap, God is immediately incensed. Abraham is, at most, corrected, but Sarah is plainly punished. Why this disparate behavior on the part of the Lord? Once again, we would attribute this to the mind of the narrator, rather than the Lord. For in the storyteller's eyes Sarah is being highly disrespectful to Abraham, the angels, and the Lord. Abraham, on the other hand, is involved in covenant talk, a business deal, and his behavior is more acceptable.

There does appear to be a surprising amount of equality between Sarah and Abraham. She appears to say what she wants, when she wants, and Abraham at times responds in almost meek obedience. He does not command her; she commands him, yet there seems to be an affectionate bond between them. Abraham does not abandon Sarah during her barrenness, nor does he gain other wives while she lives, as far as we know. The two have grown up together and grown old together, and when Sarah dies, Abraham can do nothing but weep. Sarah is a matriarch of the first order: respected by rulers and husbands alike, a spirited woman and bold companion.

Reading

Genesis 11:29–31	18:1–15
12	20
16	21:1–21
17:1–21	23:1, 2, 19

Lot's Daughters

> And the first-born said to the younger, "Our father is old, and there is not a man on earth to come in to us after the manner of all the earth. Come, let us make our father drink wine, and we will lie with him, that we may preserve offspring. . . ."
>
> (Genesis 19:31, 32)

Among the stories of Sarah, Abraham, and Hagar comes the strange tale of Lot and his family, and the destruction of Sodom and Gomorrah. After the tent conversation with the angels, God tells Abraham that the cities of Sodom and Gomorrah will be destroyed, "for their sin is very grave." Abraham bargains with the Lord: will you indeed destroy the righteous with the wicked? he asks. What if there are fifty righteous people there? God says if fifty are there, fifty will be spared, and Abraham continues to bargain until God agrees to ten. "For the sake of ten I will not destroy it," says the Lord, and God and Abraham go their ways.

Following this, two angels come to Sodom in the evening. Lot, Abraham's nephew, is sitting in the gate. He rises, bows, and invites the strangers to spend the night at his house. After some hesitation, they agree, and Lot prepares a feast for them. But before they lay down to sleep, all the men of the city, both young and old, surround the house. They call to Lot: "Where are the men who came to you tonight? Bring them out to us, that we may know them." The Jerusalem Bible records "that we may abuse them." "Know" refers to sexual relations, in this instance, homosexual. Lot responds to the men by going out the door and shutting it behind him:

> I beg you, my brothers, do not act so wickedly. Behold, I have two daughters who have not known man; let me bring them out to you, and do to them as you please; only do nothing to these men; for they have come under the shelter of my roof.
>
> (Genesis 19:7, 8)

There follows a scuffle with Lot and the city men, and the door almost breaks. The angels inside rescue Lot, and the men outside are struck with a blindness.

The angels tell Lot to gather his family, for they are about to destroy the city. Morning dawns, and Lot is reluctant to leave, but the angels seize him, his wife, and daughters by the hand, and place them outside Sodom. The angels part with a warning:

> Flee for your life; do not look back or stop anywhere in the valley; flee to the hills lest you be consumed. (Genesis 19:17b)

Lot and his family flee, and the Lord rains brimstone and fire on Sodom and Gomorrah. But Lot's wife, as she travels behind, looks back, and she becomes a pillar of salt.

Lot now lives with his daughters in a cave outside the small town of Zoar. The daughters, thinking all men on earth have been destroyed, decide to sleep with their father so they might have children. They ply him with wine, and on consecutive nights have intercourse with him. The scripture then reports that "both the daughters of Lot were with child by their father." The firstborn daughter bears a child named Moab, who becomes father of the Moabites; the younger bears a son named Ben-ammi, father of the Ammonites.

The story of Lot's family again allows us to see into the culture and mind of early Israel. Lot's behavior with the city men, however abhorrent, makes clear the importance of daughters in the community. Lot is not as concerned with his daughters' welfare as he is with obliging his guests. According to ancient laws of hospitality, once guests had eaten in a house, the host would guarantee them protection. Lot's honor extended to these men, yet his daughters held little worth, even though they were his only children. The scripture, however, indicates him as one of the "righteous" remaining.

We note further the namelessness of the daughters and wife. Whereas sons, uncles, and fathers are usually named, the women are not. Lot's wife and daughters remain anonymous to us, as do Noah's wife and daughters, and countless more. This namelessness bothered scholar and activist Elizabeth Cady Stanton, writing in the 1890s:

> Then as now names for women and slaves are of no importance: they have no individual life, and why should their personality require a life-long name? Today the woman is Mrs. Richard Roe, tomorrow Mrs. John Doe, and again Mrs. James Smith according as she changes masters, and she has so little self respect that she does not see the insult of the custom.[4]

The stories themselves are very ancient myths and should not be taken literally. The story of Lot's wife turning back was most likely a tale told to account for some unusual salt formations in this particular region. Just so, the following incident of Lot's daughters in the cave was a story told to explain the origin of the Moabites and Ammonites, neighbors of Israel.[5] But once again, in the stories themselves, we can see subtle prejudices on the writer's part. It is Lot's wife, not Lot, who turns back and is destroyed, as she has less importance. And Lot's daughters, who are actually attempting to be resourceful in their shattered world, are painted in shady colors: incest was forbidden by the Law (cf. Leviticus 18:6–18), and the story therefore becomes a gibe at Israel's foes. The writer mocks the Moabites and Ammonites, and Lot's daughters are put to shame. Yet underlying the story is the sisters' essential despair concerning offspring. Their worth, it seems, could only be valued with productivity.

Reading
Genesis 18:16–33
19

Rebekah

> Before he had done speaking, behold, Rebekah, who was born to Bethuel the son of Milcah, wife of Nahor, Abraham's brother, came out with her water jar upon her shoulder. The maiden was very fair to look upon, a virgin, whom no man had known.
> (Genesis 24:15, 16)

Rebekah's story opens with a description of Abraham: Abraham is old, advanced in years, and he calls his servant to him. Put your hand under my thigh, he says, and swear by the Lord that you will not take a wife for my son, except she be from my kindred. The servant agrees to avoid all Canaanite women, and he goes off to the city of Nahor, in search of a wife for Isaac.

The servant arrives, with ten camels and choice gifts, at a well outside the city.

> And he made the camels kneel down outside the city by the well of water at the time of evening, the time when women go out to draw water. (Genesis 24:11)

The servant prays to the Lord that the maiden who gives him drink and waters his camels will be Isaac's future wife. Before he finishes his prayer, Rebekah comes; she is young and beautiful. The servant asks for water, which she gives him, and then she draws for his camels also. While she does this, the man gazes at her in silence, to discern whether or not she is the Lord's appointed. He then gives her a ring for her nose and bracelets for her arms and asks whose daughter she is. The daughter of Bethuel, she replies, and the man bows his head:

> Blessed be the Lord, the God of my master Abraham, who has not forsaken his steadfast love and faithfulness . . . .
>
> (Genesis 24:27)

Rebekah is indeed a kinswoman, second cousin to Isaac, and she runs to tell her mother's household. Laban, her brother, and Bethuel, her father, hear the servant's story: they welcome him and give him permission to take Rebekah. The servant in turn gives Rebekah silver and gold jewelry and clothing, and to her mother and brother costly ornaments. Rebekah and her maids leave with the servant the following morning; the family blesses her as she goes:

> Our sister, be the mother of thousands of ten thousands; and may your descendants possess the gate of those who hate them!
>
> (Genesis 24:60)

Rebekah and Isaac later meet in a field in the evening. Isaac goes to meditate, and he sees camels coming. Rebekah alights from her camel, Isaac takes her to his tent, she becomes his wife, and, the story says, he loves her.

Abraham, in the meantime, has married a woman named Keturah, and they have six sons. Abraham then dies and leaves all that he has to Isaac. Isaac and Ishmael bury him in the cave of Machpelah, with Sarah. For some time after this Rebekah and Isaac live together, but Rebekah is barren. Isaac prays to the Lord and Rebekah conceives: she gives birth to twins, both sons: the firstborn is red and hairy, named Esau, and the second son, born holding onto the heel of the first, is named Jacob. Jacob grows to be a quiet man, a shepherd, while Esau is a skillful hunter, a man of the field. Rebekah loves Jacob, and Isaac loves Esau.

One day Esau comes in from the field, feeling famished, and he sells his birthright to Jacob for a bowl of pottage. With this begins the family quarrel. Jacob, whose name means "supplanter" continues to outdo Esau, with the help of his mother Rebekah. Isaac is now old, his eyesight dim, and he feels he is to die. He calls Esau to him, asking that he prepare "savory food such as I love," that he might eat and bless Esau, before he dies.

Rebekah, hearing the conversation, goes quickly to Jacob: she instructs Jacob to take Esau's place, that he might receive the blessing. Jacob protests:

> Behold, my brother Esau is a hairy man, and I am a smooth man. Perhaps my father will feel me, and I shall seem to be mocking him, and bring a curse upon myself and not a blessing.
>
> (Genesis 27:12, 13)

Rebekah is not moved: upon me be your curse, she says, only obey my word. Jacob does as he is told. While Esau is hunting, Rebekah prepares the savory food, and then dresses Jacob in Esau's clothing. She places goat skins on his hands and neck, so he will appear hairy.

Isaac is eventually tricked, although he suspects that something is amiss: "the voice is Jacob's voice," he says, "but the hands are the hands of Esau." Are you really my son Esau? he asks, and Jacob answers, yes. Isaac gives his blessing, just as Esau enters. Esau cries out when he discovers the deception, and Isaac gives him a blessing also.

Now Esau, says the story, hates Jacob and wants to kill him. After his father dies, Esau thinks, he will kill his brother. But Rebekah hears of this, and goes to Isaac: Esau has previously married a Hittite woman, and Rebekah uses this as argument. "I am weary of my life because of the Hittite woman," she says; "if Jacob marries one, what good will my life be?" Then Isaac charges Jacob: you shall not marry one of the Canaanite women. He sends him to the house of Bethuel, Rebekah's father, and tells him to take one of Laban's daughters for a wife. Jacob then goes to Laban, his mother's brother, and in doing so, he avoids the wrath of Esau.

The story of Rebekah, as it unfolds, begins with a certain idyllic quality. The description at the well is one of scripture's finest; we are immersed with camels, bells, water, pitchers, and the sheer romance of it, yet Elizabeth Cady Stanton is indignant with the scene:

> Why did not Laban and Bethuel draw the water for the household . . . . It was certainly a good test of her patience and humility to draw water for an hour, with a dozen men looking on at their ease, and none offering help. The Rebekahs of 1895 would

> have promptly summoned the spectators to share their labors, even at the risk of . . . matrimonial alliance.

Stanton further comments that milkmaids and drawers of water, with pails and pitchers on their heads, are always far more attractive to men than women with votes in their hands, or rule in their government.[6]

Rebekah, we would have to say, does not stay innocently beautiful long, for she grows from the water-girl into a powerful, influential matriarch. It is interesting to note the writer does not judge her behavior; he simply tells her story. Her influence over Jacob and Isaac is evident: both seem to do her bidding, with little or no protest. Rebekah appears to be a master of intrigue, and has learned well to have her way. She is strong and daring and bold, not at all cast in a submissive mold, her spirit willful and very much alive.

Reading

Genesis 24
25:1–6, 19–34
27
28:1–10

Leah and Rachel

> Now Laban had two daughters; the name of the older was Leah and the name of the younger was Rachel. Leah's eyes were weak, but Rachel was beautiful and lovely. (Genesis 29:16, 17)

Jacob goes on his journey, and comes to the land of the people of the east. He sees a well in a field, with many sheep lying beside it, and a large stone on the well's mouth. Shepherds are also there, and Jacob speaks with them about his uncle Laban. Do you know him? he asks them; they reply yes, and turn to show him Rachel, Laban's daughter, coming with the sheep:

> Now when Jacob saw Rachel the daughter of Laban his mother's brother, and the sheep of Laban . . . Jacob went up and rolled the stone from the well's mouth, and watered the flock . . . . Then Jacob kissed Rachel, and wept aloud. (Genesis 29:10, 11)

Jacob tells Rachel that they are kin, and she runs to tell her father.

Laban, in turn, runs to meet Jacob: he embraces him, kisses him, and brings him home. "Surely you are my bone and my flesh!" Laban says to Jacob, and Jacob stays a month. At the end of this time, Laban asks what Jacob's wages will be; Jacob replies he will serve seven years for Laban's younger daughter Rachel. Leah, the older daughter, has "weak eyes" but Rachel is beautiful and lovely, and Jacob loves her.

So Jacob serves the seven years, in place of a bride price, but at the end of that time Laban tricks him: Laban prepares an elaborate wedding feast, but in the evening he gives Jacob his daughter Leah. As Leah is veiled, Jacob doesn't discover the ruse until the next day: "And in the morning, behold, it was Leah." The two men argue: What have you done? says Jacob, incensed; Laban replies that in his country, the firstborn daughter is given before the younger. Complete the marriage festivity for this one, he says, and we will give you the other one also—for seven more years of work. Jacob now has two wives, and several more years of servitude.

Jacob loves Rachel the more, but Leah is prolific. The two sisters begin a race for sons: Leah immediately bears Reuben, Simeon, Levi, and Judah. When Rachel sees her own barrenness she shouts at Jacob: "Give me children, or I shall die!" Jacob is angry and says that he is not God. Rachel then gives him her maid, Bilhah, who in turn bears Dan and Naphtali. Leah gives Jacob her maid, Zilpah; she bears Gad, meaning "good fortune!" and Asher, meaning "happy am I!" The tally now stands six sons for Leah, and two for Rachel.

Some time after this one of Leah's sons, Reuben, finds mandrakes in a field. As mandrakes were prized as an aphrodisiac, the sisters begin to haggle over them: Rachel wins the mandrakes, but as payment Leah hires Jacob for an evening. She then bears Issachar, and after him, another son, Zebulun. The story further notes, in one sentence, that Leah also has a daughter, called Dinah. God finally remembers Rachel; she gives birth to Joseph, saying "may the Lord add to me another son!" Leah is now credited with eight sons, Rachel three, for a total of eleven sons, and one daughter.

Jacob now asks Laban permission to take his family and go home. Laban refuses, but asks Jacob to name his wages. The men continue to plot and counterplot against one another until Jacob outsmarts Laban: with ancient trickery Jacob produces many striped and spotted animals, which then become his own, according to an earlier deal. He steadily grows wealthy in Laban's own sheep and goats.

Trouble begins to brew: Laban's sons see Jacob's deception, and murmur among themselves. The Lord tells Jacob to leave, and Jacob calls Rachel and Leah to him: "I see that your father does not regard me with favor as he did before," he says, and proceeds to call Laban a cheat. Jacob says God has told him to return to the land of his birth, and the sisters concur:

> Is there any portion or inheritance left to us in our father's house? Are we not regarded by him as foreigners? For he has sold us, and he has been using up the money given for us.
> (Genesis 31:14, 15)

The decision is made, the livestock are gathered, and Rachel, Leah, Jacob, the maids, and children mount their camels to leave. Laban has gone to shear his sheep, and in a last act of defiance, Rachel steals the household gods. "And Jacob," says the story, "outwitted Laban the Aramean . . . ." The family flees.

Hearing the news three days off, Laban pursues for a week. He finally overtakes the burdened company:

> What have you done, that you have cheated me, and carried away my daughters like captives of the sword? Why did you flee secretly, and cheat me, and did not tell me, so that I might have sent you away with mirth and songs, with tambourine and lyre?
> (Genesis 31:26, 27)

Laban ends his tirade with a final question: Why did you steal my gods? Jacob, not realizing Rachel has stolen them, replies that whoever has the gods will die. Laban proceeds to hunt for them. He looks in Jacob's tent, Leah's tent, and the maids' tent, but does not find them. Rachel, in the meantime, has taken the gods, put them in her camel's saddle, and is presently sitting on them. Laban feels all about her tent, too, but cannot find his treasure. Rachel says to him:

> Let not my Lord be angry that I cannot rise before you, for the way of women is upon me. (Genesis 31:35)

Using menstruation as an excuse, Rachel outwits her father, for if she is unclean, the saddle, too, is unclean, and he cannot touch it.

Laban never finds the gods, and he and Jacob continue their lengthy argument. "What is my offense? What is my sin, that you have hotly pursued me?" shouts Jacob. Laban retorts that the daughters are his, the children are his, and the flocks are his. The men finally wear one another down: they bury their differences, gather stones for a heap, and make a covenant, calling the pillar "Mizpah," or watchpost. "The Lord watch between you and me, when we are absent one from the other," says Laban; God is witness.

Laban returns home; the family continues on. Jacob sends messages ahead to his brother Esau, whom he has not seen in twenty years. The messengers return, saying Esau is coming to meet him, along with four hundred men. Jacob, afraid and distressed, sends presents. That night he takes his wives, his maids, and his eleven children, and crosses the river Jabbok. Jacob stays on the far side of the river, where he wrestles all night with an angel. The angel changes his name to Israel, meaning "he who strives with God."

The next day Jacob sees Esau coming and he divides the family for battle in order of importance: the maids and their children first, Leah and her children, then Rachel and Joseph. But Esau runs to meet Jacob: he embraces him, kisses him, and they weep. The brothers are reconciled, and Jacob is once again home.

We last hear of Rachel sometime later. The family is journeying to Bethel, to make an altar to God. Rachel is pregnant for the second time, and her labor is hard. While she is in labor the midwife says to her: "Fear not, for now you will have another son." As Rachel dies in childbirth, she names her son Benoi, meaning "son of my sorrow." But Jacob calls him Benjamin, "son of the right hand." Rachel is buried on the way to Ephrath and Jacob sets a pillar on her grave.

The story of Rachel, Leah, Jacob, the children, and Laban is one of love, hate, fear, anger, jealousy, and strife. Yet this extended family, in the middle of quarrels and reconciliations, manages somehow to survive together. Rachel and Leah are almost eclipsed by the excitement of the story itself, yet we can still discern several things about their personalities and positions.

The race for sons is paramount in its importance, of such great weight that Rachel declares she will die if she does not have them. Indeed she does die bearing Benoi, the son of her sorrow, yet even then he seems to have greater worth. Elizabeth Cady Stanton comments:

> In Rachel's hour of peril the midwife whispers sweet words of consolation. She tells her to fear not, that she will have a son, and he will be born alive. Whether she died herself is of small importance so that the boy lived. . . . The dying wife gasps a name for her son, but the father pays no heed to her request, and chooses one to suit himself.[7]

However we interpret the different sentiments involved here, it is clear that the son is of great importance. The one daughter of all the children, Dinah, is introduced in almost an aside. She is also left out of the counting when the family crosses the ford at Jabbok: for there are twelve children then, but only the eleven sons are mentioned.

One further note is Rachel and Leah's attitudes towards their father. They are, for all purposes, still his property as they still live in his household. Their rebellion against him, then, carries no little weight, as he controls their destinies. It is with great abandon on their parts that they agree to leave and go to a foreign land, and it is with total abandon that Rachel steals the gods. According to ancient custom the gods insured a man's leadership of the family and his claim on the property. In effect, Rachel takes the power into her own hands.

Rachel further institutes this power by sitting on the camel saddle to guard the gods. Leviticus describes at some length bodily discharges which produced ritual uncleanness. In part, the passage states:

> When a woman has a discharge of blood which is her regular discharge from her body, she shall be in her impurity for seven days, and whoever touches her shall be unclean until the evening. And everything upon which she lies . . . shall be unclean; everything also upon which she sits shall be unclean.
>
> (Leviticus 15:19, 20)

Rachel, knowing she would be unclean, turns this into a positive force. For with her menstruation she holds power. This incident raises subtle and volatile questions of the blood taboo: What is there to fear? Why is this shameful? Could not blood, the life-giving force, be so powerful an image that it carries inherent threat? Our story does not tell us. We must also keep in mind that there is a double layer of prejudice here: the narrator, while assuming Rachel's uncleanness, is also ridiculing the foreign idols upon which she sat. For the idols are enemies to the God of Israel, and Rachel's blood would render them defiled. This is a joke on the writer's part, at the expense of a woman.

We have to admire Leah and Rachel for their forthrightness. No shrinking violets here. These women, these matriarchs, are once again bold, daring, and astounding in their lack of obedience. Fathers and husbands may have rule, but the women have power, and they use it to best advantage.

With Leah and Rachel the history of the legendary matriarchs comes to a close. Far from conforming to a traditional servitude, these women grace the pages of Genesis with their laughter, their sorrows, their strength, and their power.

Reading

Genesis 29
30
31
32
33
35:16–29

Although the great family stories have been told, there yet remain a few smaller stories of women of the tribe of Jacob, before moving to the tales of Egypt and the Exodus. Dinah and Tamar are included in these, Dinah being the only daughter of Leah and Jacob, and Tamar being the wife of one of Judah's sons. The stories appear among the tales of the twelve brothers.

Dinah

> Now Dinah the daughter of Leah, whom she had borne to Jacob, went out to visit the women of the land; and when Shechem the son of Hamor the Hivite, the prince of the land, saw her, he seized her and lay with her and humbled her.
>
> (Genesis 34:1, 2)

Jacob and his brother Esau have been reconciled, and Jacob and his family now live near the city of Shechem, in the land of Canaan. Dinah, Leah's only daughter, goes out one day to visit some of the Canaanite women. The prince Shechem sees her, seizes her and lays with her. His "soul is drawn to Dinah"; he loves her and speaks tenderly to her. Shechem speaks with his father, Hamor: "Get me this maiden for my wife."

Hearing of the defilement of his daughter, Jacob gathers his sons, who have been in the fields; the sons are indignant, and very angry. Hamor, Shechem's father, comes to speak with them:

> Make marriages with us; give your daughters to us, and take our daughters for yourselves. You shall dwell with us; and the land shall be open to you; dwell and trade in it, and get property in it. (Genesis 34:9, 10)

Shechem also pleads: I will give you whatever you ask, he says, only give me the maiden to be my wife.

The brothers answer that they cannot give their sister to "one who is uncircumcised," for it would be a disgrace. But if you and all your males will be circumcised, they say, then we will consent. We will give you our daughter, and we will take your daughters; but if they will not be circumcised, we will take our daughter and be gone.

Hamor and Shechem are pleased, and agree to the bargain. They return to their city and speak to their people, persuading them that the sons of Jacob are friendly:

> Will not their cattle, their property and all their beasts be ours? Only let us agree with them, and they will dwell with us.
> (Genesis 34:23)

The people listen to Hamor and Shechem, for they are princes and honored men. Accordingly, all the males are circumcised, and the agreement is sealed.

Three days later, while the men are yet sore, Simeon and Levi, Dinah's brothers, come upon the city secretly and kill all the males with their swords. Hamor and Shechem are slain, and Dinah is taken from Shechem's house. The sons of Jacob then plunder the city, taking flocks, herds, children, wives, and wealth. Jacob says to Simeon and Levi: you have brought trouble on me. He worries about a counterattack; his household, he says, will be destroyed. The brothers respond:

> Should he treat our sister as a harlot? (Genesis 34:31)

With the last remark the story ends, and Dinah is once more brought into focus. Dinah's story is one of shame: she is raped, bargained for, and passed from one clan to another. We hear relatively little of her, but a great deal of property, cattle, and trading. The politics of the bargaining overshadows the woman herself, and the story seems to reflect more continuing communal battle than anything else. The Israelites and Canaanites once again clash over territory and property, and Dinah appears to be excuse enough for a feud. Of Dinah's feelings in the entire matter we know nothing.

It is of interest that the RSV story heading calls this "the seduction of Dinah." Seduction implies that Dinah had a part or at least a choice in the matter, yet the story itself gives no indication of this. Dinah is raped: Shechem "seized her and lay with her and humbled her." The verb here usually translated as humble, *'inna*, indicates moral and social degrading and debasing; the young woman would lose expectancy of a fully valid marriage.[8]

The story, in its original intent and purpose, most likely had little to do with an actual Dinah. Using the guise of individuals, the story portrays relations between the Canaanite city and early Hebrew tribes. The violent actions of Simeon and Levi reflect events which forced these particular tribes to leave the area and gradually decline in power.[9] Yet we are struck that the oral story which preceded this, and the writer himself, chose to portray a woman as cause of, and carrier of, shame. The rape is symbolic in that it is Israel who is misused, yet it is the figure of a woman who remains unclean. Dinah appears to us as a shrouded figure: defiled, spoiled, unclean, unable to cleanse herself from this violent act.

Reading
Genesis 34

Tamar

> And when Tamar was told, "Your father-in-law is going up to Timnah to shear his sheep," she put off her widow's garments, and put on a veil, wrapping herself up, and sat at the entrance to Enaim . . . . (Genesis 38:13, 14a)

The story of Tamar and Judah comes in between the stories of Rachel's son Joseph and his brothers. Judah, one of the twelve brothers, is now a grown man. He marries a Canaanite woman, the daughter of Shua, and they have three sons: Er, Onan, and Shelah. Judah takes a wife for Er, his firstborn; her name is Tamar.

Er, described as "wicked in the sight of the Lord," is slain by the Lord. Judah says to Onan, the second son:

> Go into your brother's wife, and perform the duty of a brother-in-law to her, and raise up offspring for your brother.
> (Genesis 38:8)

But Onan, thinking the children would not be his, spills his semen on the ground when he has intercourse with Tamar, so not to credit his brother with offspring. The Lord is displeased, and Onan is also killed. Judah tells Tamar to remain a widow in her father's house until the youngest son Shelah grows up; he secretly fears that this son, too, will die. Tamar then goes to live with her father.

After a time Judah's wife dies. After Judah is comforted, he goes to Timnah to his sheepshearers. Tamar is told that her father-in-law is going to shear his sheep, and she sheds her widow's clothing. She veils herself, wraps herself up, and sits on the road to Timnah:

> . . . for she saw that Shelah was grown up, and she had not been given to him in marriage. (Genesis 38:14b)

Judah sees her, takes her for a cult prostitute, and approaches: Come, let me come in to you, he says. Tamar asks him what he will give her in return, and Judah says a goat from his flock. Tamar presses for a pledge, asking for his signet, cord, and staff, until the promised payment arrives. Judah agrees; they have intercourse, and Tamar conceives. Tamar then goes home and puts on her widow's garments.

Judah later tries to send the goat in payment. He asks a friend to look for the "harlot," but the woman is nowhere to be found. Judah decides to let her keep his pledges, lest he be laughed at. About three months later Judah is told that Tamar his daughter-in-law has "played the harlot," and further, she is with child. Judah's response is immediate: "Bring her out, and let her be burned."

As Tamar is brought for burning, she sends word to her father-in-law: "By the man to whom these belong, I am with child." She then produces the signet, the cord, and the staff. Judah acknowledges them as his own, and says:

> She is more righteous than I, inasmuch as I did not give her to my son Shelah. (Genesis 38:26)

Tamar lives to bear twin sons, Perez and Zerah, and here the story ends.

The story of Tamar and Judah is striking. The tale begins with the ancient custom of levirate marriage: according to this, the duty of a brother-in-law was to produce a male descendant for his deceased brother; the brother's name and inheritance would then continue. Deuteronomy 25:5–10 describes this process, instructing the woman involved not to marry outside the family. The passage continues to say that if the brother-in-law refuses, the woman can complain to elders of the city. If the brother-in-law still refuses:

> . . . then his brother's wife shall go up to him in the presence of the elders, and pull his sandal off his foot, and spit in his face . . . . And the name of his house shall be called in Israel, the house of him that had his sandal pulled off. (Deuteronomy 25:9a, 10)

Levirate marriage was serious agreement for the women of Israel, for their worth in the family structure depended on male heirs. Tamar, therefore, has a desperateness about her: Er is gone, Onan is gone, and Shelah is not available. In her desperation she sets a trap for her father-in-law, who does exactly as she wishes. Her future is now assured, her familial rights established. Tamar's story is rarely told. Elizabeth Cady Stanton refers to it only as "unworthy"[10] due to its moral implications. The fact that Judah would so casually visit a "prostitute," following his wife's death, seems to cause no stir. Also overlooked is the fact of Tamar posing as a cult prostitute. According to Merlin Stone in *When God Was a Woman,* the women connected with the temple of the Goddess were not at all "prostitutes" as the writers of Israel portrayed them. They were revered, often well-to-do married women whose sexual activity paid tribute to the Goddess:

> Among these people the act of sex was considered to be sacred, so holy and precious that it was enacted within the house of the Creatress of heaven, earth and life.[11]

Tamar does not pretend to be a harlot as we think of it, but rather a married woman who indulges in this practice.[12]

Yet Tamar is usually judged, in her disguise, as a totally shameful person. It would seem, however, from the story, that Judah is the erring one, and indeed the story itself does support Tamar. Judah is portrayed as avoiding Tamar as best he can. But Tamar is not one to quietly live out perpetual widowhood: she gathers her wits about her, waits for a time, then acts. Her plan is risky indeed, for she has nothing less than her life to lose. Yet she would rather die than live without the promise of heirs. Says scholar Gerhard Von Rad:

> To understand Tamar's act, the reader must resist comparing it with modern conditions and judging it accordingly, for the modern world has nothing that could be compared with it. In the ancient Orient, it was customary in many places for married women to give themselves to strangers because of some oath. Such sacrifices of chastity in the service of the goddess of love, Astarte, were, of course, different from ordinary prostitution even though they were repulsive to Israel.[13]

For a woman having no recourse, Tamar refuses to be fooled or forgotten. The writer of this story rightly gives her praise.

Reading

Genesis 38
Deuteronomy 25:5–10

TWO

Women of the Exodus

1. Bold wife of Pharaoh's Captain of the Guard, who unsuccessfully propositions Joseph. **2.** Woman who gives birth to Moses; places him in basket among reeds for a princess to find. **3.** One of the seven daughters of Jethro, priest of Midian; becomes wife of Moses. **4.** Woman prophet who leads victory song and dance at Sea of Reeds; celebrated sister of Aaron and Moses. **5.** Five daughters who request the property of their dead father; take their case before Moses and the people.

We now continue with the Jacob story and follow the family of Israel as they become captives in Egypt. With this bondage begins the great tale of the Exodus and the wilderness wanderings leading to the promised land.

Potiphar's wife

> Now Joseph was handsome and good-looking. And after a time his master's wife cast her eyes upon Joseph, and said, "Lie with me." (Genesis 39:6c, 7)

The account of Potiphar's wife and Joseph comes during Joseph's stay in Egypt, when he serves the Pharoah. Joseph, Rachel's son, is cast as the hero, while Potiphar's wife, a nameless Egyptian woman, is the temptress. This story follows the Tamar-Judah episode of Chapter 1, but we must turn back to gather lost details.

Rachel has died at the birth of Benjamin, and after this Jacob's father Isaac also dies. Rachel's first son, Joseph, is Jacob's favorite:

> Now Israel loved Joseph more than any other of his children, because he was the son of his old age; and he made him a long robe with sleeves. (Genesis 37:3)

Joseph's "coat of many colours" is a luxurious robe, different from the ordinary sleeveless tunic which reached to the knees. When Joseph's brothers see that their father loves him above the others, they hate him. Further, they "can not speak peaceably to him."

Joseph has a dream. But when he tells his brothers of it, they hate him all the more. In the dream, he says, we were binding sheaves in the field:

> . . . and lo, my sheaf arose and stood upright; and behold, your sheaves gathered round it, and bowed down to my sheaf.
> (Genesis 37:7)

The brothers are incensed: are you to reign over us? they say; are you to have dominion over us? Then Joseph dreams another dream, and once again tells his brothers: this time, he says, the sun, the moon, and eleven stars were bowing down to me. Joseph also tells his father of the dream. Jacob rebukes Joseph, but keeps the saying in his mind. The brothers' jealousy grows.

The brothers go to pasture their father's flock near Shechem. Jacob sends Joseph to join his brothers, asking him to see if all is well. Joseph goes after his brothers; the brothers see him coming, from a distance, and conspire to kill him:

> Here comes this dreamer. Come now, let us kill him and throw him into one of the pits; then we shall say a wild beast has devoured him, and we shall see what will become of his dreams.
> (Genesis 37:19, 20)

Brother Reuben disagrees: let us not take his life, he says; shed no blood, but cast him into a pit. Reuben secretly hopes to rescue Joseph.

Joseph comes. They strip him of his elegant robe and cast him in a pit. The pit is empty, and without water.

The brothers then sit down to eat. Looking up, they see a caravan of Ishmaelites, with camels bearing gum, balm, and myrrh: they are on their way to Egypt. Judah turns to his brothers:

> What profit is it if we slay our brother and conceal his blood? Come, let us sell him to the Ishmaelites . . . .
>
> (Genesis 37:26, 27a)

They lift Joseph from the pit and sell him to the traders for twenty shekels of silver. The caravan continues to Egypt.

Reuben returns to the pit, having evidently been away, to find Joseph missing. He tears his clothes: "The lad is gone, and I, where shall I go?" The other brothers take Joseph's long robe, kill a goat, and dip the robe in blood. They then take this to their father, Jacob. Jacob is undone:

> It is my son's robe; a wild beast has devoured him; Joseph is without doubt torn to pieces. (Genesis 37:33)

Jacob tears his clothes, puts on sackcloth, and mourns his son; he refuses to be comforted.

Joseph, in the meantime, has been sold in Egypt to Potiphar, an officer of Pharoah, and captain of the guard. The Lord is with Joseph, says the story, and he becomes successful. Potiphar makes Joseph overseer of his house, and puts him in charge of all that he has. Potiphar's house prospers.

Now Joseph, says the story, is handsome and good-looking. After a time the wife of Potiphar entreats him: "lie with me." But Joseph refuses, saying this would be "great wickedness." Potiphar's wife persists, speaking to Joseph day after day; Joseph continues to refuse. One day, when everyone is gone from the house, the Egyptian woman catches Joseph by his clothing, saying "lie with me." Joseph flees, leaving his clothing in her hand.

Potiphar's wife thinks fast: she tells the men of her household that Joseph tried to force her, and she shows the garment as proof. When her husband comes home she tells him the same story, and Potiphar's anger is kindled. He takes Joseph and puts him in prison with the king's prisoners. Joseph remains there for some time. But the Lord is with Joseph, says the story, and he soon is in the favor of the keeper of the prison.

In contrast to the Tamar-Judah tale, the woman in this story is clearly the villain. The writer's main purpose is to hold up Joseph as undefiled, innocent, loyal. Potiphar's wife, on the other hand, is rather the opposite: she is consumed with a passion, she is clever, she is daring. Her story has long been a scandal. She has been called evil, wicked, sensual, spoiled, and selfish.[1] Whichever of these is true, one thing is certain: she is a determined woman. We must admit there is not much to say favorably of Potiphar's wife, at least according to this writer's version of the story. A well-known ancient Egyptian "Story of the Two Brothers" relates a striking parallel, in which a wife attempts to seduce the younger brother.[2] The woman is again portrayed as treacherous, and she is later killed. With our story we must keep in mind that the narrator favors Israel, and a foreign woman would of course be suspect. Joseph, on the other hand, can do no wrong, and is continually in the Lord's favor.

We mention this entertaining little story to add to the flow of family history—for now the people of Israel change lands. During his stay in prison, Joseph interprets Pharaoh's dreams, and eventually he is made a ruler of Egypt. Joseph and his father and brothers are finally reunited in Egypt, and there they live in comfort and splendor. But time passes: Joseph and his brothers die, Pharaoh dies, and an entire generation disappears. But the descendants of Israel continue to grow and multiply, filling the land of Egypt. A new king rises in Egypt, one who does not remember Joseph.

> And he said to his people, "Behold, the people of Israel are too many and too mighty for us. Come, let us deal shrewdly with them . . ." (Exodus 1:9, 10a)

The people of Israel, once highly honored, now become slaves, and with this we begin the story of the Exodus.

Reading

Genesis 37
39
40–50 (Joseph history)

Jochebed and Zipporah

> Amram took to wife Jochebed his father's sister and she bore him Aaron and Moses . . . (Exodus 6:20)

> But Moses fled from Pharaoh, and stayed in the land of Midian; and he sat down by a well. Now the priest of Midian had seven daughters . . . . And Moses was content to dwell with the man, and he gave Moses his daughter Zipporah. (Exodus 2:15b,21)

The story of Moses and the people of Israel begins in Egypt. The new Pharaoh dislikes the Israelites, and forces them into hard labor. He sets taskmasters over them to afflict them with heavy burdens: they build for him the stone cities of Pithom and Raamses. But, says the story, the more the Israelites were oppressed, the more they multiplied.

Pharaoh speaks with two midwives of Israel, Shiphrah and Puah:

> When you serve as midwife to the Hebrew women, and see them upon the birthstool, if it is a son, you shall kill him, but if it is a daughter, she shall live. (Exodus 1:16)

But the midwives fear God, and do not obey Pharaoh's wishes; they let all the male children live. Pharaoh calls the midwives: why have you done this? he demands. The midwives tell him Israel's women are too vigorous; they deliver children before they can arrive. Pharaoh commands that every son shall be cast into the Nile; but the people multiply, and grow strong.

We next hear of the birth of a child: a woman conceives, bears a son, and hides him for three months. When she can no longer hide him, she takes a basket made of bulrushes, puts the child in it, and places it among reeds at the river's brink. The child's sister stands at a distance, watching. Pharaoh's daughter comes with her serving women to bathe at the river. She sees the basket, fetches it, and opens it to find the child. This is one of the Hebrews' children, she says, and she takes pity on the child. The sister appears: Shall I call a nurse from the Hebrew women for you? she asks the princess. The sister then goes to call the child's mother. The woman comes, takes the child, and nurses him. The child grows and becomes a son to Pharaoh's daughter; she names him Moses, for he has been drawn out.

One day, when Moses is grown, he sees an Egyptian beating an

Israelite. Thinking no one sees him, he kills the Egyptian, hiding him in the sand. The next day he sees two Israelites fighting and he tries to stop them. One says: Who made you a prince and judge over us? Do you mean to kill me as you killed the Egyptian? Moses is afraid. Pharaoh hears the story, and seeks to kill him.

Moses flees Egypt, and goes to the land of Midian, where he sits by a well. The seven daughters of the priest of Midian come to draw water. Shepherds come to drive them away, but Moses stands to help them water the flock. They return to their father, Reuel, and tell him the story. Where is he? Reuel asks; call him, that he may eat bread. Moses then lives with the priest, and Reuel gives him his daughter Zipporah. She bears a son, calling him Gershom, sojourner.

The daughter Zipporah appears only once again in a strange incident some time later. By now Moses has seen God in the flame of fire, the burning bush. God calls Moses to return to his people in Egypt and Moses goes, after much hesitation. He takes his wife and children, "sets them on an ass," and begins the journey home. On the way they stop at a lodging place where "the Lord met him and sought to kill him." Zipporah takes a flint, cuts off her son's foreskin, and touches Moses' "feet" with it, this being a euphemism for sexual organs. Surely you are a bridegroom of blood to me! she says. Moses escapes the incident unharmed. Zipporah vanishes from the remainder of the Moses story, except for a brief incident when Moses sends her and their sons back to Midian. They meet once again in the wilderness, when Moses leads the people from Egypt.

The Moses story is disappointing in that we know so little of the women involved. Jochebed, the mother of Moses, is mentioned only twice by name in scripture, and in the birthing story she remains nameless. Miriam, also, the sister of Moses, is at the first only referred to as "sister." Her brothers are mentioned by name, but only later do we know the sister as Miriam. Pharaoh's commands concerning daughters and sons reflect the worth of females: daughters are of such little account that they may live, while all the sons must die.

Zipporah, too, remains a shadowy figure. We know her only as the daughter of the priest and mother of sons. Later, in the bizarre and unaccountable incident of the flint and the foreskin, she appears to save Moses' life from an unnamed demon. Of her personality, we know nothing. Clearly the writer's intention is to focus on Moses, the hero of Israel, yet we would have wished for more detail of the women who bore him, cared for him, and raised his sons. At least we see in the two brave midwives, Shiphrah and Puah, some of the boldness of the women of Israel.

Reading

Exodus 1
2
3–4 (Moses and the Lord)
4:18–26

Miriam

> Then Miriam, the prophetess, the sister of Aaron, took a timbrel in her hand; and all the women went out after her with timbrels and dancing. (Exodus 15:20)

Once again we hear of Miriam. This time she appears at the crossing of the sea of reeds, when the Israelites foil the armies of Pharaoh. In this instance Miriam is called "prophetess" as she sings and dances before the Lord.

Before this great event, the people of Israel have been in long bondage: Moses returns from his exile in Midian to find great affliction. He and his brother Aaron speak with Pharaoh, asking him to let the people go. Pharaoh refuses:

> Moses and Aaron, why do you take the people away from their work? Get to your burdens. (Exodus 5:4)

Pharaoh commands his taskmasters to no longer give the people straw for making bricks, and he calls for heavier work. The people blame Moses and Aaron for their troubles; Moses in turn complains to God: Why did you ever send me? he asks. God reassures Moses:

> Now you shall see what I will do to Pharaoh; for with a strong hand he will send them out, yea, with a strong hand he will drive them out of the land. (Exodus 6:1)

A series of ten plagues follows: blood, frogs, gnats, flies, cattle plague, boils, hail and thunderstorm, locusts, thick darkness, death of the first-born. With each plague Pharaoh promises to free the people, then hardens his heart against them. Pharaoh continues to refuse Moses and Aaron, until the passing of the angel of death. Moses gathers the people before this final plague: he tells them to kill the passover lamb and dip a bunch of hyssop in its blood. Then, he says, touch the lintel and two doorposts with the blood. They are not to leave the house until morning. For the Lord will pass through to slay the Egyptians, but the destroyer will pass by the doorposts of blood. You and your children shall observe this rite forever, says Moses, when you come to the land which the Lord has promised:

> "And when your children say to you, 'what do you mean by this service?' you shall say, 'It is the sacrifice of the Lord's passover, for he has passed over the houses of the people of Israel in Egypt, when he slew the Egyptians but spared our houses.' " And the people bowed their heads and worshipped. (Exodus 12:26,27)

So the people of Israel go to their houses, and at midnight the first-born are slain: from Pharaoh's son to prisoners' sons to cattle. Pharaoh rises in the night and hears a great cry, for the dead are everywhere. He summons Moses and Aaron: Go, serve the Lord, he says; take your flocks and your herds and be gone. And bless me also! The people bind up their mixing bowls, their jewelry, and clothing, and they go.

God leads the Israelites into the wilderness with a pillar of cloud by day and a pillar of fire by night. They journey to the sea of reeds. Pharaoh, changing his mind, pursues them with horses and chariots and horsemen and army; the Egyptians overtake the Israelites as they are encamped at the sea. The people see Pharaoh coming, and they cry to Moses: Is it because there are no graves in Egypt that you take us to die in the wilderness? What have you done to us? Moses says to the people:

> Fear not, stand firm, and see the salvation of the Lord, which he will work for you today; for the Egyptians whom you see today, you will never see again. (Exodus 14:13)

Moses stretches out his rod over the sea and the Lord drives the sea back with a strong east wind. The waters divide, and the people of

Israel go into the midst of the sea, on dry ground. The Egyptians pursue, with all their horses, chariots, and horsemen, and the entire army is drowned. But, says the story, the people of Israel walk on dry ground, the waters being a wall to them on their right hand, and on their left.

Then the people rejoice: they sing a song of victory. Miriam takes a timbrel, and all the women follow her with timbrels and dancing. Miriam sings to them:

> Sing to the Lord, for he has
> triumphed gloriously;
> the horse and his rider he has thrown
> into the sea.
>
> (Exodus 15:21)

The wondrous story of the Exodus culminates in The Song of Miriam, an ancient song of triumph.

Miriam appears again, much later in the Moses story. By this time the people have journeyed far into the wilderness. They survive thirst, famine, and attack. God supplies them with quail and manna, yet they constantly complain. They cry to Moses, and Moses prays to the Lord. Miriam and Aaron, also, speak against Moses: they criticize him for marrying a foreign woman, and they resent his authority:

> Has the Lord indeed spoken only through Moses? Has he not spoken through us also? (Numbers 12:2)

The Lord hears this and calls the three to the tent of meeting. The Lord comes down in a pillar of cloud and is angry with Aaron and Miriam: Moses is my servant, says the Lord; with him I speak mouth to mouth. When the Lord leaves and the cloud disappears, Miriam is leprous, white as snow.

Aaron pleads with Moses: do not punish us, he says, and Moses cries to the Lord: Heal her, O God. But the Lord replies to Moses:

> If her father had but spit in her face, should she not be shamed seven days? Let her be shut up outside the camp seven days, and after that she may be brought in again. (Numbers 12:14)

This is the last we hear of Miriam, save for a brief mention of her death at Kadesh, in the wilderness of Zin.

Miriam begins triumphantly and fades into disgrace and obscurity. She stands out clearly as a prophet, in the earliest sense of the word. Her ecstatic singing and dancing before the Lord cause her to win the title of prophet, and enhance her leadership and charisma. Much later in the history of Israel we encounter prophecy of a similar nature when Samuel anoints the young Saul king. Saul joins a wandering band of prophets who prophesy with harp, tambourine, flute, and lyre. The spirit of the Lord comes upon Saul; he prophesies with them, and "turns into another man." (cf. I Samuel 10:1–13)

Miriam is this same prophet, and she is no less than a king. She is indeed turned into another as she leads her women in a song of victory. The Song of Miriam, as it is called, is one of the oldest poetic couplets in the Old Testament, and was probably composed by an eyewitness of the event.[3] Yet chapter headings often label this "The Song of Moses," referring to the lengthier version in Exodus 15, and including Miriam's song. Miriam's song is the older of the two, yet Moses receives the credit.

Miriam seems also a leader equal to her brothers, as evidenced by a passage from the prophet Micah:

> For I brought you up from the land
> of Egypt,
> and redeemed you from the house
> of bondage;
> and I sent before you Moses,
> Aaron, and Miriam.
>
> (Micah 6:4)

Women are rarely named as tribal figures or national heroines, yet Miriam seems to carry a good deal of influence in her community. It is of great interest, then, that Miriam is the one to receive leprosy, in the minor mutiny against Moses, while Aaron remains untouched. Perhaps this suggests the kind of power Miriam held, and perhaps to the storyteller this seemed dangerous.

Miriam's punishment is severe, and though her brothers defend her, the Lord appears to be particularly harsh, both with the leprosy, and with the implication of a curse. Being spat upon by a father is the sign of a curse, and God says the punishment cannot be less than this shame.[4] This is indeed quite curious. The narrator, rather than the Lord, seems to have a particular bias against Miriam. Her name is listed before Aaron's in the mutiny story; this is unusual and suggests a certain blaming emphasis on the woman.

Elizabeth Cady Stanton comments:

> As women are supposed to have no character or sacred office, it is always safe to punish them to the full extent of the law. So Miriam was not only afflicted with leprosy, but also shut out of the camp for seven days.[5]

Edith Deen, however, sees Miriam differently:

> The limitations in Miriam's character come into clear focus . . . This time she is a leader in jealousy and bitterness . . . . The foul vice of envy had spread over her whole character, like the loathsome disease which had overtaken her.[6]

The text does not seem to suggest this strong a statement against Miriam. It does suggest that she held influence, and that the people followed her. We would raise these—her power and her charismatic leadership—as possibilities for her demise. Had she been a brother such as Aaron, most likely she would have lived to look over the mountain into the promised land, rather than dying an early death in the wilderness.

Reading

Exodus 5–14 (plagues, passover, deliverance)
  15:20,21 (Miriam's song)
Numbers 11 (the people's complaint)
  12 (Miriam and Aaron mutiny)
  20:1 (death of Miriam)
Micah 6:3,4 (Miriam as leader)

Daughters of Zelophehad

> Now Zelophehad the son of Hepher had no sons, but daughters: and the names of the daughters of Zelophehad were Mahlah, Noah, Hoglah, Milcah and Tirzah. (Numbers 26:33)

The story of Moses and the people in the wilderness would be incomplete without the tale of five young women, the daughters of Zelophehad. Mahlah, Noah, Hoglah, Milcah, and Tirzah have a rarity about them, for in a time when daughters had few privileges, they ask for the right to their deceased father's property.

The wilderness story continues as the people, weary from years of wandering, near the promised land. Moses sends ahead spies to the land of Canaan. The spies return, saying the land "flows with milk and honey," but the people who dwell there are strong, and the cities fortified. The people are as giants, they say, and we ourselves like grasshoppers.

The people weep all night from fear. They speak against Moses and Aaron, saying, "Would that we had died in Egypt!" Only Joshua and Caleb, two of the chosen spies, speak favorably of the land. But the congregation wants to stone them, so they will be silenced. The glory of the Lord then appears to all the people: the Lord is veiled, but the people see the light of holy presence. The Lord is angry and wants to disinherit Israel for its unbelief, but Moses pleads for pardon. The people will be pardoned, says the Lord, but no one over twenty years will enter the new land, save Joshua and Caleb. Further, God says they must wander forty more years in the wilderness. The people repent.

Time wears on, and the people continue to fight and skirmish within and without the camp of Israel. Three men, Korah, Dathan, and Abiram, rebel against Moses and Aaron; they gather hundreds about them, saying to the leaders:

> You have gone too far! For all the congregation are holy, every one of them, and the Lord is among them; why then do you exalt yourselves above the assembly of the Lord? (Numbers 16:3)

Moses arranges a meeting with them the following morning, and at that time the earth splits and swallows the rebels. Hundreds more are consumed by fire.

The story continues with further disasters: plagues, deaths, warring, and serpents. The people defeat several kings of Canaan as they draw closer to the promised land. After a time a census is taken to measure the strength of the tribes, and to allot the land. Sons of all the tribes are listed, daughters not being counted. A man named Zelophehad, however, has no sons, but five daughters. The daughters are listed by name, under their father's title.

Moses and the priest Eleazar number the people as they come forward to be counted. The daughters of Zelophehad—Mahlah, Noah, Hoglah, Milcah, and Tirzah—stand before Moses, Eleazar, and the entire congregation. They say:

> Our father died in the wilderness; he was not among the company of those who gathered themselves together against the Lord in the company of Korah, but died for his own sin; and he had no sons. Why should the name of our father be taken away from his family, because he had no son? Give to us a possession among our father's brethren. (Numbers 27:3,4)

Moses brings their case before the Lord, and the Lord says the daughters of Zelophehad are right. You shall give them possession of an inheritance among their father's kin, says the Lord, and cause the inheritance of their father to pass to them. Moses writes a law to this effect, and the daughters win their case.

But the story continues. Some time after, the male heads of the houses in Zelophehad's tribe gather. They speak with Moses, expressing discontent over the new law favoring daughter's inheritance. If the daughters marry out of our own tribe, they say, then their inheritance will go to another tribe; the inheritance should remain in the tribe of our fathers. Moses consults the Lord again, and the Lord makes a new command:

> Let them marry whom they think best; only, they shall marry within the family of the tribe of their father. (Numbers 36:6b)

The daughters do as the Lord commands Moses and marry sons of their father's brothers. Their inheritance remains in the tribe of their father.

The story of the daughters is both delightful and disappointing. The delight lies in the apparent outspoken manner of the five women. They do not hesitate to stand in front of Moses, the priest, and the entire congregation to ask for what is rightfully theirs. This was unprecedented in the history of Israel. According to ancient law, a woman had no property rights and would therefore not inherit anything belonging to her father. Sons and brothers received the land. The daughters, then, make an astounding request: give to us a possession among our father's kin.

The next surprising and equally astounding occurrence is that the Lord says they are right. This is possibly the only instance where the Lord, in the mind of the narrator, sides with a woman. And five of them at that. A further refreshing development is that Moses writes the request into law: the daughters' request becomes a statute and an ordinance. The small tale of the daughters is full of surprises, and leaves us cheering the consequence.

But lest we think the victory permanent, the story reverses in an almost predictable way. The fathers gather in their troubled state, and once again the fate of the daughters goes up for counsel. This time the Lord defers to the men, while leaving the women their property. The earnest and humorous closing statement of the Lord reflects the minds of all concerned. The daughters are allowed some rights, but not too many.

Elizabeth Cady Stanton comments on the gathering of the fathers:

> They seemed to consider these noble women destitute of the virtue of patriotism, of family pride, of all the tender sentiments of friendship, kindred and home, and so with their usual masculine arrogance they passed laws to compel the daughters of Zelophehad to do what they probably would have done had there been no law to that effect.[7]

Regardless of the compromised outcome, Mahlah, Noah, Hoglah, Milcah, and Tirzah are delightful indeed, for they dare to enter a territory previously sanctioned for men.

Reading

Numbers 13 (spying out the land)
14 (the Lord and the people)
16 (rebellion)
20–25 (plagues and warrings)
26 (census)
27:1–11 (daughters)
36 (fathers)

THREE

Women of the Promised Land

1. Woman "harlot" who hides Joshua's spies at Jericho; she and family are later saved by scarlet cord tied in window. **2.** Only woman judge of Israel; prophet, counselor, and warrior, much loved by her people. **3.** Tribal heroine who drives a tent peg into the head of Sisera, an opposing general. **4.** Young woman who sacrifices herself for her father's vow; bewails her virginity on the mountainside. **5.** Philistine woman bribed by her countrymen to discover Samson's great strength.

We have seen that the books of Exodus and Numbers contain the Moses story: the journey of the people of Israel from Egypt through the great wilderness, and finally, to the promised land of Canaan. As they near the river Jordan, the Lord speaks to Moses:

> Say to the people of Israel, when you pass over the Jordan into the land of Canaan, then you shall drive out all the inhabitants of the land from before you, and destroy all their figured stones, and destroy all their molten images, and demolish all their high places; and you shall take possession of the land and settle in it, for I have given the land to you to possess it.
>
> (Numbers 33:51–53)

The story then goes on to describe the boundaries of the land: Canaan is to be bordered by wilderness in the south, sea in the west, mountains in the north, and river in the east. The people, says the Lord, are to inherit the land by lot according to their families. Eleazar the priest and Joshua the young leader are appointed to divide the land.

The book of Deuteronomy is essentially an extended address by Moses to the people, something of a historical review, and a farewell. Moses remembers where they began and where they have come: he speaks of victories and defeats, and most especially, of the Lord who delivered and sustained them. He recounts the people's sins, rebellions, and complaints. He calls for obedience to the Lord God of their ancestors. He recites once again the great Commandments of the Lord, and further instructs the people:

> Hear, O Israel: The Lord our God is one Lord; and you shall love the Lord your God with all your heart, and with all your soul, and with all your might. And these words which I command you this day shall be upon your heart; and you shall teach them diligently to your children, and shall talk of them when you sit in your house, and when you walk by the way, and when you lie down, and when you rise. (Deuteronomy 6:4–7)

This is the great *Shema*, meaning "hear," one of the most noted passages in the Old Testament.

The discourse continues with various instructions and warnings. Moses recounts again and again the miracle at the sea of reeds: remember, he says, the Lord your God, who brought you out of Egypt with great signs and wonders. The core of this history is found in another notable passage, an ancient creedal recital of the mighty acts of the Lord:

> A wandering Aramean was my father; and he went down into Egypt and sojourned there, few in number; and there he became a nation, great, mighty, and populus. And the Egyptians treated us harshly, and afflicted us, and laid upon us hard bondage. Then we cried to the Lord the God of our fathers, and the Lord heard our voice, and saw our affliction, our toil, and our oppression; and the Lord brought us out of Egypt with a mighty hand and an outstretched arm, with great terror, with signs and wonders; and he brought us into this place and gave us this land, a land flowing with milk and honey. (Deuteronomy 26:5–9)

And with this recital Moses calls the people to repentance. He tells them to be strong and of good courage, for they are about to enter the promised land. Moses then appoints Joshua as his successor, and gives the people song and blessing. At the end of the book of Deuteronomy God tells Moses to climb Mount Nebo, and there view Canaan, the land of promise. Moses does so, and then he dies. The people bury him in a secret place, and mourn and weep for him thirty days. Joshua, "full of the spirit of wisdom," takes command, and we are left with an epigraph for Moses, the servant of the Lord:

> And there has not arisen a prophet since in Israel like Moses, whom the Lord knew face to face, none like him for all the signs and wonders which the Lord sent him to do in the land of Egypt, to Pharaoh and to all his servants and to all his land, and for all the mighty power and all the great and terrible deeds which Moses wrought in the sight of all Israel.
>
> (Deuteronomy 34:10–12)

Rahab

> And Joshua the son of Nun sent two men secretly from Shittim as spies, saying, "Go, view the land, especially Jericho." And they went, and came in to the house of a harlot whose name was Rahab, and lodged there. (Joshua 2:1)

We now move, in the history of Israel, to the conquest of the land of Canaan. The book of Joshua begins with God telling Joshua and the people to go over the Jordan into the land. "Every place that the sole of your foot will tread upon I have given to you," says the Lord. Joshua tells the people to prepare; the time has come. He then sends spies to the city of Jericho, and tells them to "view the land." They go, and find lodging in the house of Rahab, a prostitute. In the meantime, word has reached the king of Jericho that spies are in the city. He sends to Rahab, asking her to give up the men of Israel. Rahab feigns ignorance: true, she says, some men came to her house, but they left at dark. If you pursue them quickly, she suggests, perhaps you will overtake them. The king's men leave in haste, and chase imaginary foes to the fords of the Jordan.

Rahab goes up to her roof, where she has hidden the spies under stalks of flax. She tells them she knows of their reputation and of their God—how this Lord has given them the land, how the Lord dried up the water for them, how they defeated the Amorite kings.

> And as soon as we heard it, our hearts melted, and there was no courage left in any man, because of you; for the Lord your God is he who is God in heaven above and on earth beneath.
> (Joshua 2:11)

Appealing to their mercy, she asks for asylum for herself and her entire family when the people of Israel take Jericho. "Our life for yours!" the men respond, and they promise to deal kindly and faithfully with her when the time comes. Rahab then lets the men down by a scarlet rope through the window, as her house is built into the city wall. She tells them to hide in the hills, and they in turn tell her to bind the scarlet cord in the window, and gather her family into one house. They swear allegiance to one another, and part. Rahab binds the cord in the window.

The spies return safely to Joshua, and the people camp by the river Jordan. Joshua tells them to sanctify themselves, "for tomorrow the Lord will do wonders among you." The Levite priests carry the ark of the covenant before the people, the ark being a holy vessel for the presence of the Lord. The Lord assures Joshua of victory, and the crossing of the river begins. The priests go first, carrying the ark, and as they step into the Jordan the waters "rise up in a heap" and the people pass over on dry ground. The Lord tells Joshua to take twelve stones from the Jordan and set them up as a memorial to the passing of the people of Israel.

> . . .when your children ask in time to come, what do these stones mean to you?" Then you shall tell them that the waters of the Jordan were cut off before the ark of the covenant of the Lord.
> (Joshua 4:6, 7a)

The people camp in Gilgal, on the east border of Jericho, and there they set up the stones.

The Lord next instructs Joshua to march around the city of Jericho for six days. The ark will go before them, and the priests are to bear rams' horns, and blow them on the seventh day:

> And when they make a long blast with the ram's horn, as soon as you hear the sound of the trumpet, then all the people shall shout with a great shout; and the wall of the city will fall down flat. . . . (Joshua 6:5)

The people do as the Lord commands them and on the seventh day they rise at dawn to march again. Joshua calls out "Shout; for the Lord has given you the city." The priests blow the trumpets, the people raise a great shout, and the walls of Jericho come tumbling down.

Joshua says that only Rahab the harlot and all her household shall live, for it was she who hid the messengers of Israel. He tells the two spies to go to her house and bring out her entire family. Rahab, her father, mother, brothers, and relatives are then brought outside the camp of Israel, while the city burns. Jericho is captured and destroyed, and the people of Israel triumph.

Rahab is one of the few Old Testament women who is also mentioned several times in the New Testament. She is mentioned there three separate times, by three different writers. The writer of the Gospel of Matthew includes her in the opening genealogy: ". . . and Salmon the father of Boaz by Rahab." If this is true, then evidently Rahab was accepted by the people of Israel and married into the community. Her son Boaz was later to marry Ruth, the Moabite. Rahab is also listed among the faithful in Hebrews 11, the great faith chapter: "By faith Rahab the harlot did not perish with those who were disobedient, because she has given friendly welcome to the spies." Sarah is the only other woman mentioned in the naming of the faithful. And finally, she is also referred to by the writer of James, who speaks of faith versus works: "You see that a man is justified by works and not by faith alone. And in the same way was not Rahab the harlot justified by works when she received the messengers and sent them out another way?" (James 2:24, 25)

Almost every time we hear mention of Rahab, she is called "Rahab the harlot." Edith Deen makes an interesting comment on this: Josephus, a Jewish historian during the first century, and some of the early rabbis refer to Rahab not as a harlot, but as an innkeeper. Deen further notes that, according to her sources, persons who kept inns were not always the most moral; sometimes they were called harlots.[1] This raises the question of Rahab's character and profession. It is interesting to speculate that Rahab may have been an unmarried woman who ran her own business — a place where strangers would naturally come for lodging. A woman such as this would be very rare in these ancient times, and could easily have been looked upon as suspect or labeled a harlot. This could very well be biased speculation, but we have to keep in mind that the writers of the narratives also held their own conscious and unconscious prejudices. "Rahab the harlot" could just as easily be "Rahab the innkeeper." Regardless, she stands in history as one of the faithful: a clever woman, politically astute, who later became a noted personage in the annals of Israel.

Reading

Joshua 1:1–11
2
3
4
6

Deborah and Jael

> Now Deborah, a prophetess, the wife of Lappidoth, was judging Israel at that time. She used to sit under the palm of Deborah between Ramah and Bethel in the hill country of Ephraim; and the people of Israel came up to her for judgment.
> (Judges 4:4–6)

> But Sisera fled away on foot to the tent of Jael, the wife of Heber the Kenite; for there was peace between Jabin the king of Hazor and the house of Heber the Kenite. And Jael came out to meet Sisera, and said to him, "Turn aside, my lord, turn aside to me; have no fear." (Judges 4:17, 18)

We now move from the book of Joshua to the book of Judges. In order to understand the rise of the great judges of Israel, we must first glance back to see what has happened since the burning of Jericho.

Rahab and her family are saved. The Israelites go on to conquer other parts of the land, and they are defeated at Ai, a city on a high mountain ridge. The people blame the defeat on a man named Achan, who has stolen some forbidden gold, silver, and a beautiful mantle from Jericho. The Lord is angry, Achan confesses, and he and his entire family are stoned and burned: sons, daughters, oxen, asses, sheep. The Israelites again attack Ai, and this time they conquer; they hang the king of Ai on a tree, and build an altar to the Lord.

Hearing of the destruction of Jericho and Ai, other kings of the land band together: Hittites, Amorites, Canaanites, Perizzites, Hivites, and Jebusites. All except the Gibeonites, who devise a clever plan. These people, fearing the power of Israel, dress as those from afar, and ask for peace:

> . . . they on their part acted with cunning . . . and took worn-out sacks upon their asses, and wineskins, worn-out and torn and mended, with worn-out patched sandals on their feet, and worn-out clothes; and all their provisions were dry and moldy.
> (Joshua 9:4, 5)

They trick Joshua and the others into making a covenant with them: look at our moldy bread and worn-out garments, they say; we have come on a very long journey. Joshua makes peace with them, and three days later hears the truth: the Gibeonites are neighbors. But an oath once taken cannot be broken, so the Gibeonites become hewers of wood and drawers of water for the congregation of Israel.

Soon after this, five kings of the Amorites gather forces against the people of Gibeon. The Gibeonites appeal to Joshua for help: "Do not relax your hand from your servants; come up to us quickly, and save us, and help us." So Joshua and the people go, and there is a great slaughter at Gibeon, with the Amorites fleeing from Israel. Joshua commands the sun and moon to stand still, and Israel is victorious. The five kings hide in a cave, but they are captured, humiliated, and hung upon trees until evening.

After the Gibeonite incident, Joshua proceeds to move south. He lays siege to the whole of southern Canaan, and is victorious over all. Hearing the news, the northern Canaanite kings band together, but Joshua defeats them, too, in his blaze through the northern territory. The land is then distributed among the people of Israel, each tribe having certain boundaries. Cities of refuge are appointed for those who kill someone unintentionally. The people begin to settle into the land, and at the end of the book of Joshua, Joshua himself makes a farewell address. He calls the people together, and tells them to be faithful to Moses' commandments and to love and serve the Lord. He warns them against apostasy, and promises future victories.

Before his death, Joshua renews the covenant between God and Israel at Schechem, where all the tribes have gathered. Joshua says he is "about to go the way of all the earth," and he leaves the people with a final request:

> Now therefore fear the Lord, and serve him in sincerity and in faithfulness; put away the gods which your fathers served beyond the River, and in Egypt, and serve the Lord. And if you be unwilling to serve the Lord, choose this day whom you will serve . . . but as for me and my house, we will serve the Lord.
> (Joshua 24:14, 15)

The people answer, "Far be it from us that we should forsake the Lord, to serve other gods.[2] Joshua makes a covenant with the people, sets up a great stone near an oak, and sends the people off to their lands. Then he dies, and Eleazar the priest also dies, and a new age begins.

It must be noted that the book of Joshua views the entire conquest of Canaan as miracle. The writer, reflecting back into history, attributes victories to the work of the Lord rather than military prowess. Thus we have the Lord throwing down great stones upon enemies, burning and stoning, and intervening with the natural courses of sun and moon. Much of this is poetry and exaggeration, and these acts of violence cannot necessarily be claimed as the Lord's work. Nevertheless, the point to be made—minus the writer's national fervor—is that the people of Israel did indeed feel the intimate presence of Yahweh, the Lord: the holy one whose name was never spoken, but whose aid was most assuredly present.

The book of Joshua would lead us to believe that the conquest of Canaan was achieved in a brief series of campaigns under the leader Joshua. In actuality, this is probably not so. We know from the following book of Judges that many parts of the country remained unconquered, and battles were fought for several generations before Israel owned the land. Rather than a *blitzkrieg*, then, as the Joshua writer portrays it, we have an actual historical process, taking some time. Different tribes, perhaps, came into the region slowly, and eventually Israel did indeed reign.

The book of Judges presents a consistent picture of the patterns of Israel: apostasy, judgment, repentance, restoration. The people would be unfaithful to the Lord, captured and defeated by various foes; then they would repent, and God would raise up for them a judge. The judges were probably tribal heroes—minor kings of a sort, who held what power they could for a time. The first three of these judges were men: Othniel, Ehud, Shamgar. Each one of these people appeared when Israel forgot God; the judges would then exhort the people to faithfulness, defeat the current enemy, and rule in peace for varying years. One of these small stories, the story of Ehud and Eglon, the king of Moab, holds some interest.

Ehud the judge is left-handed. He goes to Eglon the Moabite and feigns tribute. Now Eglon, says the scripture, is a very fat man. Ehud tells the king he has a secret for him, and Eglon sends the people away.

Ehud says he has a message from God: he reaches for his sword, with the unsuspected left hand, and thrusts it into the king's belly. The sword goes in, hilt and all, and the fat closes over the blade. Eglon the king repairs to his private closet and the guards think he is relieving himself. They finally find him dead on the floor, and Israel once again is victorious. We mention this small tale not for its violence but for the humor it is meant to portray; the writers of Israel, in times of war, always seem to enjoy a good laugh on their foes.

The fourth judge is a woman, and a prophet at that. She is Deborah, one of the most remembered of the judges. About this time, the people of Israel are being oppressed by Jabin, king of Canaan. Jabin lives in Hazor and has an army commanded by a man named Sisera. Deborah is presently judge in Israel; the scripture pictures her as sitting under a palm in the hill country, with the people coming to her for counsel. She is introduced as a "prophetess" and "wife of Lappidoth," but we know nothing of why she has earned the title of prophet, nor do we hear anything of her husband. Perhaps one of the few women not defined by her husband, Deborah stands clearly on her own.

The story opens with Deborah sending a message to Barak, her chief of command. She says that the Lord commands him to gather his troops and meet Sisera, the opposing general. Barak's response is one to remember:

> Barak said to her, "If you will go with me, I will go; but if you will not go with me, I will not go." And she said, "I will surely go with you; nevertheless, the road on which you are going will not lead to your glory, for the Lord will sell Sisera into the hand of a woman." (Judges 4:8, 9)

Deborah's comment sets the stage for the emergence of another woman, Jael. But Jael's time has not yet come, so off go Deborah and the faint-hearted Barak to meet the foe. Sisera, in the meantime, calls out nine hundred chariots of iron, and all his men. The two forces meet at Mount Tabor, and Deborah has to encourage Barak every step of the way:

> Up! For this is the day in which the Lord has given Sisera into your hand. Does not the Lord go out before you?
> (Judges 4:14a)

Barak takes up the charge with ten thousand men following, and the Canaanites are duly routed from the field. Sisera jumps from his chariot and flees on foot.

Sisera runs unwittingly from one woman to another. He reaches the tent of Jael, the wife of Heber the Kenite. Supposedly there is peace between her tribe and his, and she greets him with words of assurance: have no fear, she says, turn aside to me. He enters her tent and she covers him with a rug. Sisera then asks for a drink and Jael gives him some milk from a skin. He further instructs her to not let anyone know of his whereabouts, then falls asleep from weariness. While he sleeps, Jael takes a hammer and a tent peg and drives the peg into his temple. Sisera dies. Jael then goes to meet Barak, who is pursuing, and she shows him the dead general. The people of Israel rejoice in yet another victory.

Following this narrative is what is known as the "Song of Deborah," a long poem which recounts the deeds of Deborah, Barak, and Jael. This happens to be the oldest remaining fragment of Hebrew literature. The song has been composed about Deborah, not by her. Deborah is referred to as "mother in Israel" and Jael is praised alike:

> Most blessed of women be Jael,
> the wife of Heber the Kenite,
> of tent-dwelling women most
> blessed.
>
> (Judges 5:24)

The song goes on to describe in detail how Jael brought down Sisera. The song, having exalted both women as national heroines, ends with a summary couplet:

> So perish all thine enemies,
> O Lord!
> But thy friends be like the sun as
> he rises in his might.
>
> (Judges 5:31)

Deborah and Jael are most certainly honored friends of Israel, yet we need to mention a few disparate things in connection with them. In the New Testament book of Hebrews, for instance, a strange thing occurs in Chapter 11, the faith chapter previously referred to. The writer rehearses a litany of the faithful from the time of Sarah and Abraham. Isaac, Jacob, Esau, and Moses are mentioned, and also Rahab. Next, several judges are listed: Gideon, Barak, Samson, Jephthah, then on to David and Samuel. After reading the story of Deborah and Barak, it is a bit surprising to see Barak named among the judges, while Deborah is nowhere mentioned. Here again we have a blatant bias on the part of the writer. Had Barak been in any way an equal to Deborah, there might be grounds for the omission, but it is most evident that he was a weak-kneed character needing continual encouragement from the true "mother in Israel."

Another disparate vote is voiced in a commentary by Stanton. Whereas the biblical narrative holds up Jael as a national heroine, Stanton condemns her:

> The deception and the cruelty practised on Sisera by Jael under the guise of hospitality is revolting under our code of morality. To decoy the luckless general fleeing before his enemy into her tent, pledging him safety, and with seeming tenderness ministering to his wants, with such words of sympathy and consolation lulling him to sleep, and then in cold blood driving a nail through his temples, seems more like the work of a fiend than a woman.[3]

Stanton here seems to be caught in a trap: she is moralizing, and does not see the apparent double standard. In the history of Israel, male heroes and national figures are continually slaying thousands, Saul and David being prominent examples:

> And the women sang to one another as they
> made merry,
> "Saul has slain his thousands,
> and David his ten thousands."
> (I Samuel 18:7)

This is not to say this kind of behavior is admirable, but it is distressing to see a woman criticized for what would be the expected male norm, among the warriors of Israel. Jael surpasses Barak in her notoriety, and it is fitting, in the context of the story, that she should be a praiseworthy figure.

Following the story of Deborah, Barak, and Jael is a brief story worth mentioning. Deborah reigns in peaceful times for forty years, and God then raises up another judge, Gideon. The people have been unfaithful and are captured by the Midianites. They repent, and Gideon delivers the people by destroying an altar of Baal, the Canaanite god. After defeating the kings of Midian, Gideon comes on peaceful times. The narrative says Gideon has many wives, and he fathers seventy sons. One of the sons is named Abimelech.

Gideon soon dies, and the people of Israel turn once again to the gods of Baal. Abimelech goes to his mother's kin and persuades them that he should reign instead of his seventy brothers. They give him silver; he hires "worthless and reckless fellows" who then slay the sons of Gideon. Abimelech rules for a time, but soon he is warring with his neighbors, the people of Shechem. Fierce fighting ensues. As Abimelech prepares to burn his enemies who are holed up in a tower, a woman throws an upper millstone on Abimelech's head, crushing his skull. He is mortified that he has been assaulted by a woman:

> Then he called hastily to the young man his armor-bearer, and said to him, "Draw your sword and kill me, lest men say of me, 'A woman killed him.'" And his young man thrust him through, and he died. (Judges 9:54)

So Abimelech dies a rather ignoble death, for the woman's handiwork is the height of shame.

Reading

Joshua 7–12 (the conquest)
 23–24 (farewell and covenant)
Judges 1–3 (Othniel, Ehud, Shamgar)
 4–5 (Deborah, Barak, Jael)
 6–9 (Gideon and Abimelech)

Jephthah's daughter

> Then Jephthah came to his home at Mizpah; and behold, his daughter came out to meet him with timbrels and dances; she was his only child . . . . (Judges 11:34)

After Abimelech, two minor judges appear, Tola and Jair. Then comes Jephthah the Gileadite, described as a mighty warrior, but the son of a harlot. In his younger days, Jephthah is "thrust out" by his brothers, as they consider him a bastard by birth. Jephthah dwells in the land of Tob, and gathers about him a band of undesirable characters.

After a time Israel and the Ammonites make war. Some elders in Jephthah's previous family seek him out in the land of Tob. Come and be our leader, they say, and Jephthah responds with anger:

> Did you not hate me, and drive me out of my father's house?
> Why have you come to me now when you are in trouble?
> (Judges 11:7)

But the elders persist, and Jephthah is persuaded to lead the tribes against the invaders. Jephthah and the king of the Ammonites argue over what land belongs to whom, and Jephthah ends by saying that the Lord, the Judge, will decide between the people of Israel and the people of Ammon.

Then, says the scripture, the Spirit of the Lord comes upon Jephthah, and he makes a vow to the Lord:

> "If thou wilt give the Ammonites into my hand, then whosoever comes forth from the doors of my house to meet me, when I return victorious from the Ammonites, shall be the Lord's, and I will offer him up for a burnt offering." (Judges 11:30, 31)

With these words Jephthah goes to meet the Ammonites, and, the story reports, "he smote them . . . with a very great slaughter."

Jephthah returns home from battle, lighthearted and victorious. As he approaches, his only child, a daughter, comes to meet him with timbrels and dances. Jephthah recalls his vow, and is greatly distressed:

> And when he saw her, he rent his clothes, and said, "Alas my daughter! You have brought me very low, and you have become the cause of great trouble to me; for I have opened my mouth to the Lord, and I cannot take back my vow." (Judges 11:35)

Jephthah's daughter responds to the father she has run to meet:

> "My father, if you have opened your mouth to the Lord, do to me according to what has gone forth from your mouth, now that the Lord has avenged you on your enemies, on the Ammonites."
> (Judges 11:36)

She goes on to ask a final request: she wishes to be alone for a space of two months, that she and her friends might wander on the mountains, and bewail her virginity. Jephthah gives her a one-word assent: go.

The daugher leaves, with her companions, for her retreat in the mountains. At the end of the two months, she returns as she has promised. Her father, the story says, "did with her according to his vow which he had made." The story further describes that the daughter of Jephthah had never known a man, and it became a custom that the daughters of Israel went year by year to lament for their sacrificed sister.

This story is an example of the power of the sacred vow. In Israel, a vow was considered a *fait accompli*: if it was said, then it must be done. A man's vow was his pledge, under penalty from the Lord. But a woman's word is not weighted equally. Numbers, Chapter 30, describes vows and oaths: when a man vows, he may not break his word; but when a woman vows, the efficacy of the vow depends upon the will of her father, if she is unmarried, or her husband, if married. The men, in other words, may simply cancel or disregard the woman's vow. If the father or husband disapproves, the vow is made null and void. A widow or a divorced woman, however, can make a binding vow.

Jephthah's obedience to vow rather than emotion is astonishing, but his daughter's response is equally stunning. One would think that Jephthah's own statement might be reversed—that indeed he is the one who has caused the trouble, and he has brought his daughter very low. Stanton submits a fiery retort to the father:

> I would that this page of history were gilded with a dignified whole-souled rebellion. I would have had the daughter receive the father's confession with a stern rebuke, saying: "I will not consent to such a sacrifice. Your vow must be disallowed. You may sacrifice your own life as you please, but you have no right over mine. I am on the threshold of life, the joys of youth and middle age are all before me. You are in the sunset . . . . Better that you die than I, if the God whom you worship is pleased with the sacrifice of human life . . . . I demand the immediate abolition of the Jewish law on vows. Not with my consent can you fulfill yours." This would have been a position worthy of a brave woman.[4]

Stanton, writing in the latter part of the nineteenth century, further mentions that it was common then for people to praise the beautiful submission of self-sacrifice of the young maiden. This has also been a common twentieth-century attitude. Writing in the 1950s, Edith Deen subtitles her section on Jephthah's daughter with "Example of Noble Submission." The daughter, she says:

> ... lives on, even now ... as the embodiment of a courageous young woman who was both meek in spirit and patient in suffering.[5]

Stanton has rightly called for a whole-souled rebellion. A woman of Israel could suffer no greater disgrace than to die childless, thus the young woman's wish to "bewail her virginity." But what woman in her right mind would also willingly submit to death at her father's own hand? The story may be one of submission and obedience, but it is certainly not one to applaud. Jephthah's actions are highly offensive, and his daughter's inactions equally so. This is indeed a very human tale of misplaced loyalties and devotion. No God, as Stanton says, would require such a sacrifice. And most especially, one is left wondering what might have occurred, had the only child been a son.

Reading:
Judges 11

Delilah

> And Delilah said to Samson, "Please tell me wherein your great strength lies, and how you might be bound, that one could subdue you." (Judges 16:6)

One other story of a judge is worth mentioning, and this is the story of Samson. After the ruling of Jephthah, three more minor judges appear to help stay Israel in turbulent times. Then once again the people of Israel "do what is evil in the sight of the Lord," and they are in captivity to the Philistines for forty years. During this time we hear of a man named Manoah, married to a woman who is barren. An angel of the Lord appears to the woman and says she will conceive and bear a son. The angel warns her to avoid wine and strong drink and to eat nothing unclean. No razor shall come upon the son's head, says the angel, for the boy will be a "Nazirite to God," that is, a specially consecrated person, from the time of his birth. And further, he will deliver Israel from the Philistines.

After hearing the message, the woman, who remains nameless, goes to tell her husband the news. Then Manoah prays to the Lord:

> O, Lord, I pray thee, let the man of God whom thou didst send come again to us, and teach us what we are to do with the boy that will born. (Judges 13:8)

The angel appears to the woman once again as she sits in a field. She runs to find Manoah, and they return to the field to speak with the angel. Manoah invites the angel to eat with them, but the angel refuses; Manoah then asks the stranger's name, but the angel only says: "Why do you ask my name, seeing it is wonderful?" The angel then disappears in a flame, and the woman and Manoah fall on their faces.

Afterwards the woman bears a son and calls his name Samson. The boy grows, and the Lord, says the story, blesses him. Samson, now a young man, sees a Philistine woman who pleases him. He instructs his mother and father to "get her for me," but they object, as she is not one of their own people. But Samson's wishes prevail, and he goes to visit the woman. On his way home he sees the carcass of a lion which is filled with honey, and he scrapes some out and eats it. Later at the marriage feast Samson presents his friends with a riddle:

> Out of the eater came something to eat.
> Out of the strong came something sweet.
> (Judges 14:14)

If they guess the riddle, Samson pays them in linen and festal garments; if they cannot guess, they pay Samson. After several days of wrong guesses, the young men threaten Samson's new wife: they will burn her, and her father's house unless she tells them the riddle. She then weeps in front of Samson for seven days until Samson, weary with her pressing, tells her of the lion and honey. She in turn tells the young men, and they give Samson the answer. Samson responds:

> If you had not plowed with my heifer,
> you would not have found out my riddle.
> (Judges 14:18b)

Filled with hot anger, Samson proceeds to kill several men, take their spoil, and give festal garments to the riddle-solvers. He then returns to his father's house. We hear one line concerning the fate of Samson's bride:

> And Samson's wife was given to his companion, who had been his best man. (Judges 14:20)

The next we hear of Samson, he goes at wheat harvest to visit his former wife. Samson's marriage was evidently of the ancient kind, where the wife continued to live with her family and the husband visited on occasion. On this occasion, the woman's father will not allow Samson to see his daughter. The father explains he has given her to Samson's companion, as he thought Samson hated her. The younger sister is fairer anyway, the father suggests, and Samson might wish to take her instead. Samson does not warm to this idea; instead, he ties torches to the tails of three hundred foxes, and sends them into the fields of the Philistines. The shocks and grain burn, as well as the olive orchards, and the hapless foxes. There ensues a minor war in which the father and daughter are burned, and Samson slaughters the Philistines. The warring continues, and Samson slays a thousand men with the jawbone of an ass; his enemies try to bind him, but Samson cannot be bound.

The wondrous story of Samson builds, in which he is the invincible hero. His strength is unsurpassed: one night, as his enemies wait to kill him, Samson defies them by walking off with the gates of the city—doors, posts, bar, and all. After this he loves a woman named Delilah, a Philistine. The Lords of the Philistines come to Delilah and try to enlist her help:

> Entice him, and see wherein his great strength lies, and by what means we may overpower him, that we may bind him to subdue him; and we will each give you eleven hundred pieces of silver.
> (Judges 16:5)

Delilah does her best, but Samson misleads her; he says if he is tied with seven fresh bowstrings, he will become weak. Delilah binds him, but he snaps the bowstrings. Next he says that new ropes will hold him, but he again snaps these off, "like a thread." Then he says to weave the locks of his head; Delilah does this but is again foiled. In desperation, Delilah says to Samson:

> How can you say, "I love you," when your heart is not with me? You have mocked me these three times, and you have not told me wherein your great strength lies. (Judges 16:15)

After hearing this day after day, Samson finally succumbs: he tells Delilah that a razor has never come upon his head. If he is shaved, then his strength will leave him. Delilah makes him sleep upon her knees, and she calls someone in to shave his head. The Philistines, waiting outside, seize Samson and gouge out his eyes. Later, at a feast day for the Philistines, Samson is brought from prison to entertain the guests. His hair has begun to grow again, and while the company is merry, he gathers his strength. Samson prays to the Lord:

> O Lord God, remember me . . . and strengthen me, . . . only this once, O God, that I may be avenged upon the Philistines for one of my two eyes. (Judges 16:28)

Holding the pillars of the house, he bows with all his might, and the house comes crashing down. Thousands of people die, Samson among them. The tale ends by saying Samson judged Israel twenty years.

The story of Samson, Delilah, and the Philistines was a popular tale in ancient Israel, and has remained one of the most popular of the biblical stories. It is, in actuality, filled to overflowing with violence and horror, from foxtails to burnings to jawbones to eyes. We are left wondering where the appeal lies. Especially, one must ask: why is Samson such a hero? Delilah is most often the one to receive poor reviews. But Samson is often characterized as being "victimized" by both his first wife and Delilah, and this we would hold in question. Samson certainly does not appear to be a person of integrity. He finds sport in visiting brothels and killing enemies, and he is nowhere portrayed as a man of religious persuasions. His final prayer comes as a surprise, for nowhere previously does he show an interest in the God of his ancestors. And concerning his behavior with Delilah, we must admit he is either overcome with passion, or incredibly dim-witted. Samson and Delilah have few virtues, and this might be one story which could happily vanish from the legends of Israel. It does, however, give us an accurate, if highly exaggerated, portrayal of a typical hero of the period.

Equally so, the story also affords us a glance into the status of women. Once again we encounter the sad state of namelessness for the women of Israel. Manoah's wife, who has more dealings with the angel than Manoah, remains unnamed, other than to be called wife or mother. The angel points up the importance of a name when he refuses to reveal his because it is too wonderful. The name of a person, in Israel, held identity and revealed character, and was therefore considered holy. To the writers of the narrative, women were often too inconsequential to bear names. Not only does Samson's first wife remain nameless, but she also is passed from man to man by her father. The conversation between Samson and the father is reminiscent of a cattle or sheep exchange. Delilah at least is named, most likely for her notoriety.

Reading:
Judges 13
14
15
16

FOUR

Women of the Kingdom

1. Woman who prays for a son and is accused of being drunken; later bears Samuel and dedicates him to God. **2.** Kindly woman medium who foretells the future of King Saul. **3.** Saul's daughter and first wife of David, who becomes disenchanted with her husband the king. **4.** Woman of "good understanding" and wife of Nabal the fool, to become wife of David. **5.** Woman who bathes on the roof; wife of Uriah the Hittite, soon to become wife of David and mother of Solomon. **6.** Daughter of David; raped by her half-brother Amnon and avenged by her brother Absalom, the would-be king. **7.** Woman of Saul's harem whose sons are hanged at David's request; keeps vigil over their bodies many months.

With Delilah and Samson, we leave the book of Judges, and move further into the history of Israel. The small book of Ruth appears between Judges and I Samuel, but we choose not to include this in the history for several reasons. Although Ruth is a popular character, she is not one of the women of Israel, whom we are, for the most part, considering. Further, the book of Ruth was written much later in the history, probably a post-exilic composition, and does not therefore continue with our story line. We move, then, to the book of I Samuel, which begins the history of the kings of Israel.

The book of Judges concludes with a matter-of-fact statement:

> In those days there was no king in Israel; every man did what was right in his own eyes. (Judges 21:25)

As we have seen, this was a time of tribal judges, who later were lifted to national figures by the writers telling their deeds. No prophets are mentioned, other than Deborah, who most likely was not a national prophetic figure, but rather a tribal counselor. We come now to the first of the prophets of later times, a man named Samuel. The prophets now mentioned are not necessarily ecstatic visionaries, nor do they foretell the future; rather, they interpret the present, and hold to religious conviction of the past. Samuel is a forerunner of the first of Israel's kings, Saul, and he acts as counselor and judge.

Hannah

> As she continued praying before the Lord, Eli observed her mouth. Hannah was speaking in her heart; only her lips moved, and her voice was not heard; therefore Eli took her to be a drunken woman. (I Samuel 1:12)

I Samuel opens with a description of the birth of Samuel. There is a man named Elkanah who has two wives, Hannah and Peninnah. Peninnah has children, but Hannah has none. Elkanah, when he worships and makes his yearly sacrifice at Shiloh, gives several portions to Peninnah and her children, but only one portion to Hannah. Hannah's rival "provokes her sorely," as the Lord has closed her womb. On one such trip to Shiloh, Peninnah again agitates Hannah. Hannah begins to weep, and will not eat. Elkanah attends to her:

> Hannah, why do you weep? And why do you not eat? And why is your heart sad? Am I not more to you than ten sons?
> (I Samuel 1:8)

But Hannah is not to be consoled, and she goes to the temple of the Lord to pray. Hannah is deeply distressed, and begins to weep bitterly. She makes a vow to the Lord:

> O Lord of hosts, if thou wilt indeed look on the affliction of thy maidservant, and remember me, and not forget thy maidservant, but wilt give to thy maidservant a son, then I will give him to the Lord all the days of his life, and no razor shall touch his head.
> (I Samuel 1:11)

Eli the priest has been sitting on the seat by the doorpost of the temple. He sees Hannah's mouth moving, but hears no words, and concludes that she is a drunken woman. He interrupts her prayer to ask her how long she will be drunken, and further tells her to put away her wine. No, my lord, Hannah says, I am pouring out my soul before the Lord. She begs Eli not to regard her as a base woman, but as someone greatly vexed. Eli gives her his blessing, and prays that the God of Israel will grant her request.

The Lord remembers Hannah, and she conceives and bears a son, calling him Samuel, meaning "asked of the Lord." After a time Hannah takes Samuel to the temple, where she once again speaks with Eli. She reminds Eli who she is, and they dedicate the boy to God. Then Hannah prays a poem known as the "Song of Hannah." Following the song, the story continues: the boy Samuel is left to serve in the temple with Eli, and his parents go home. We hear twice more of Hannah: yearly, we are told, Hannah makes Samuel a "little robe" and takes it to him at the time of sacrifice. Hannah also bears three sons and two daughters. This is the last we hear of her.

Hannah is something of an undefined figure. We do know her as a woman of prayer, and something of a gentle soul. She is rarely outwardly angry, either with her rival and provoker Peninnah, or with Eli, who makes quite erroneous assumptions. Rather, she seems to be more melancholy. She also seems to fit more into the sterotype of a submissive, obedient woman; she is careful not to offend the priest, when, in reality, it is he who offends. But Hannah receives what she asks for, a son, and that is most important to her. Hannah comes at the end of a long line of women who were once barren and who bear unusual sons late in life: Sarah, Rebekah, Rachel, and the mother of Samson. Hannah is more often noted for the "little coat" she makes for Samuel, than for the beautiful song attributed to her. Hannah's song is a model for the Magnificat, Mary's Song of Thanksgiving in the New Testament. Although we hear no more of Hannah, we hear a good deal of Samuel. The story goes on to say that Samuel continues to grow in stature and favor with both the Lord and other people. The Lord speaks directly with Samuel, a rarity in those days, says the scripture, as there was no frequent vision. Samuel is now recognized by all the people of Israel as a prophet of the Lord. In the meantime, the Philistines defeat Israel and capture the ark of the covenant. Eli's sons are killed, and Eli falls dead from shock.

Samuel is now the judge of the people of Israel, and he tells them to return to the Lord. The people do so, and the Philistines are subdued. Samuel rules and peace prevails. As he ages, the people of Israel begin to demand a king:

> Behold, you are old and your sons do not walk in your ways; now appoint for us a king to govern us like all the nations.
>
> (I Samuel 8:5)

Samuel is not pleased, and the Lord is displeased as well. The Lord, however, tells Samuel to do as the people say, only warn them as well of the dangers of a king. The people persist, and Samuel goes to seek a king, the young man Saul.

Reading:

I Samuel 1
2:1–10 (Song of Hannah)
2:11–26
3–7 (Samuel and Philistines)
8 (asking for a king)

I Samuel Chapter 9 opens with a description of the young man Saul:

> There was a man of Benjamin whose name was Kish . . . and he had a son whose name was Saul, a handsome young man. There was not a man among the people of Israel more handsome than he; from his shoulders upward he was taller than any of the people. (I Samuel 9:1a, 2)

After this introduction, the story goes on to say that the asses of Kish are lost. Kish sends Saul to look for them; Saul and a servant search through many territories, but the animals are nowhere to be seen. Discouraged, Saul turns homeward, but the servant detains him. Wait, says the servant, there is a man of God in this city: let us ask him for advice. Saul and the servant ask some young girls how to find the seer, and as they enter the city, Samuel approaches them. Samuel is well aware of the strangers, for the Lord has spoken to him the day before:

> Tomorrow about this time I will send to you a man from the land of Benjamin, and you shall anoint him to be a prince over my people Israel. (I Samuel 9:16a)

Young Saul asks for the house of the seer, and Samuel invites them to stay and eat with him; the asses, he says, have been found, and there is no need to worry. Saul wonders at the preferential treatment he receives: he sits at the head of the table and is served the best portions of meat; in the evening he sleeps in comfort on a rooftop in the city.

The next morning Saul and the servant prepare to leave. The prophet Samuel sends the servant ahead and "makes known the word of God" to Saul. Taking a vial of olive oil, Samuel pours it on the head of Saul and kisses him, saying:

> Has not the Lord anointed you to be prince over his people Israel? And you shall reign over the people of the Lord and you will save them from the hand of their enemies round about.
> (I Samuel 10:1)

Thus the young man Saul becomes the first king of Israel, and Samuel sends him off to meet a band of wandering prophets. Saul joins the prophets, with their harps, tambourines, flutes, and lyres, and, the spirit of God came mightily upon him.

Another version of this story is told by a second source. In this version, Saul is chosen by lot rather than revelation. Samuel calls the people together and rebukes them for having spurned God and cried instead for a king. He tells the people to present themselves by tribes, and they do so. The young man Saul is taken by lot, after a long process of elimination, but he cannot be found. The people inquire of the Lord concerning his whereabouts, and the Lord answers: "Behold, he has hidden himself among the baggage." The people drag Saul from his hiding place, and everyone shouts: "Long live the king!"

So begins the reign of the new king. The story continues with various battles and victories, and Saul and Samuel engage in a long series of quarrels and misunderstandings. During one crucial time of warring, Saul himself sacrifices a burnt offering, in the absence of Samuel, and Samuel reprimands him harshly. Another time Saul spares the life of an opposing king, Agag; Samuel is furious, and kills the king himself. All enemies of the Lord should be utterly destroyed, he says. Samuel's rampage does not stop with the brutal death of Agag: he continues to upbraid Saul for being disobedient.

> And Samuel said to Saul, "I will not return with you; for you have rejected the word of the Lord, and the Lord has rejected you from being king over Israel." (I Samuel 15:26)

Saul and Samuel have a rather abrupt parting, and we are told that they do not see each other again until the day of Samuel's death.

This particular story is then interrupted by another search: the Lord instructs Samuel to seek out a new king, as Saul has been rejected. Samuel goes to find David, son of Jesse, a young shepherd. The cast of characters shifts to an intriguing story of Saul, his son Jonathan, David the harpist and warrior, and Michal, Saul's daughter. To this family we shall return, but we move now to the final appearance of Samuel and Saul, as they meet with the woman medium of Endor.

Woman of Endor

> Then Saul said to his servants, "Seek out for me a woman who is a medium, that I may inquire of her." And his servants said to him, "Behold, there is a medium at Endor." (I Samuel 28:7)

The scripture tells us that by this time Samuel has died. Saul is desperate: the Israelites and Philistines are about to clash once again, and Saul fears the enemies' numbers. He inquires of the Lord, but the Lord does not answer through dreams, prophets, or Urim and Thummim, sacred objects for determining divine will by lot. Saul is at a loss. He instructs his servants to find a woman medium, and they tell him of the woman at Endor.

Now Saul, the story tells us, has put all the mediums and wizards out of the land. Necessarily, then, he disguises himself and goes to see the woman at night, accompanied by two servants. He asks her to "divine for him by a spirit," and bring up whoever he names. The woman responds in fear:

> Surely you know what Saul has done, how he has cut off the mediums and wizards from the land. Why then are you laying a snare for my life to bring about my death? (I Samuel 28:9)

Saul swears that no harm will come to her, and he asks that she bring up Samuel from the dead. By this time she recognizes the king, and she is even more beside herself. She does as she is commanded, and an old man wrapped in a robe begins to rise from the depths of the earth.

Samuel is not pleased that his time in Sheol, the land of the dead, has been disturbed. He bickers with Saul, and ignores the king's distress. Saul is miserable: God has left him, he says, and he asks Samuel for advice with the Philistine matter. Samuel flashes back with, "Why then do you ask me, since the Lord has turned from you and become your enemy?" He goes on to seal the fate: the Philistines will defeat Israel, and Saul and his sons will die. On the morrow, says Samuel, you and your sons shall be with me.

Saul falls on the ground in a fit of despair, and Samuel vanishes into the night. The woman medium approaches the terrified king:

> Behold, your handmaid has hearkened to you; I have taken my life in my hand, and have hearkened to what you have said to me. Now therefore, you also hearken to your handmaid; let me set a morsel of bread before you; and eat, that you may have strength when you go on your way. (I Samuel 28:21, 22)

Saul refuses, but his servants and the woman cajole him into eating. The woman quickly kills the fatted calf she has in the house, and she bakes fresh bread as well. Saul and the servants eat and return home, late at night.

The next day the Israelites and Philistines do battle, and Saul and his sons, including Jonathan, are indeed killed. Saul is at first badly wounded by the archers, then takes his own sword and falls upon it, thus ending his life. The Philistines, upon finding the dead king, cut off his head, strip off his armor, and fasten his body to a wall. Saul's body is retrieved by loyal Israelites who steal to the wall by night and carry him away. His bones are buried under a tamarisk tree.

The story of Saul, Samuel, and the woman of Endor is brief but memorable. The first thing to be noted is that the woman is nowhere called witch. Yet over the centuries she has commonly been referred to as the "witch of Endor." The Authorized Version describes her as "a woman that hath a familiar spirit"; the Revised Standard Version calls her a "medium." But the footnotes and page headings of these versions speak of "the witch," and many commentators label I Samuel 28:3–25 as belonging to the Witch of Endor. Edith Deen describes the woman of Endor in the following manner:

> . . . a wise old person with gnarled hands, deep, penetrating eyes, course, leathery skin, and dark hair falling over her stooped shoulders. Probably she had resorted to fortune telling because

> it was her only means of livelihood . . . . many had gone to her cave home, seeking counsel.[1]

It is remarkable that this rather unassuming woman elicits such response. We do not know that she is old; we are not told she lives in a cave, has stooped shoulders, and tells fortunes. She is a necromancer, but naming her a witch is another matter. It seems that this somewhat ordinary woman has been maligned because of her unusual sight. What we do know is very little, but it can readily be seen that she is a kindly person, much more charitable than the caustic Samuel, who seems to delight in bearing ill tidings. The woman comforts Saul in his despair, and makes haste to give him the best of what she has: her calf and her bread. History has quite possibly judged her character harshly, and it would serve us well to view the woman of Endor with sympathy rather than suspicion.

Reading

I Samuel 9, 10, (the choosing of Saul)
13:5–15 (Saul's offering)
15 (Saul sparing Agag)
28:3–25 (woman of Endor)
31 (death of Saul)

Michal and Abigail

> Michal took an image and laid it on the bed and put a pillow of goats' hair at its head, and covered it with the clothes. And when Saul sent messengers to take David, she said, "He is sick."
> (I Samuel 19:13, 14)

> Now the name of the man was Nabal, and the name of his wife Abigail. The woman was of good understanding and beautiful, but the man was churlish and ill-behaved . . . . (I Samuel 25:3)

We now move back in time, when Saul and Samuel still live, and David first appears. The story of Israel's second king, David, begins when God sends Samuel on a journey:

> Fill your horn with oil, and go; I will send you to Jesse the Bethlehemite, for I have provided for myself a king among his sons. (I Samuel 16:1b)

Saul is still king, but he has lost favor in the sight of Samuel and the Lord. So Samuel goes as the Lord commands, and the elders of the city of Bethlehem come to meet him, trembling. Do you come peaceably, they ask, and Samuel assures them of good intentions. A sacrifice is arranged, and Jesse brings all his sons to this holy occasion; the sons move silently by Samuel, as he appraises them. Seven sons pass his eye, but none is the chosen one. Samuel asks Jesse if all his sons are present: Jesse replies all save one, the youngest, who is keeping the sheep. Fetch him, commands Samuel, and they wait for the remaining son. Young David comes from the fields:

> Now he was ruddy, and had beautiful eyes, and was handsome. And the Lord said, "Arise, anoint him; for this is he." Then Samuel took the horn of oil, and anointed him in the midst of his brothers; and the Spirit of the Lord came mightily upon David from that day forward. (I Samuel 16:12, 13)

The story then shifts from the anointing back to the present king Saul, who grows more and more melancholy. The Spirit of the Lord has departed from Saul, says the story, and an evil spirit torments him. Anxious for their lord, Saul's servants seek out a man skilful in playing the lyre, that his music might soothe the ailing king. The son of Jesse is mentioned to Saul, and he sends for David the shepherd. David comes, enters the king's service, and becomes his armor-bearer, and his comfort.

> And whenever the evil spirit from God was upon Saul, David took the lyre and played it with his hand; so Saul was refreshed, and was well, and the evil spirit departed from him.
>
> (I Samuel 16:23)

Another source gives us a different version of the meeting of Saul and David: during a war with the Philistines, a giant of a man appears, named Goliath. Goliath stands ten feet tall and wears a helmut of bronze and a weighty coat of mail; his legs are covered with bronze, and a javelin of bronze is slung between his shoulders. He shouts to the Israelites, taunting them. Send a man to fight with me, he says, and whoever loses will become servants of the enemy. King Saul and all of Israel are greatly dismayed.

In the meantime Jesse sends his son David to the battle, carrying loaves and cheese to his brothers. David rises early, sees his sheep are secure, and reaches the encampment in time to hear Goliath's shouts. All the men flee from the giant, but David is indignant:

> What shall be done for the man who kills this Philistine, and takes away this reproach from Israel? For who is this uncircumcised Philistine that he should defy the armies of the living God?
> (I Samuel 17:26)

David speaks with the king, and says he will fight the Philistine. Saul replies that David is but a youth, but David insists: I have killed lions and bears guarding my sheep, he says; Goliath shall be like one of them. Furthermore, he says, the Lord will deliver me. Saul says: "Go, and the Lord be with you!" Saul then clothes David in armor, but David cannot move for the weight. He sheds the armor, takes his staff and five smooth stones from the brook, and approaches the Philistine, sling in hand.

Goliath, seeing the young man, is insulted. "Am I a dog, that you come to me with sticks?" he says, and begins to curse David by his gods. "Come to me, and I will give your flesh to the birds of the air and to the beasts of the field." Unabashed, David calmly states that he comes in the name of the Lord of hosts, the God of the armies of Israel. David further says that it is he, Goliath, who will die. Running to meet the Philistine, David puts his hand in his bag, takes out a stone, slings it, and strikes a forehead blow. Goliath falls to the ground.

> So David prevailed over the Philistine with a sling and with a stone, and struck the Philistine, and killed him . . . .
> (I Samuel 17:50)

Thus David enters into Saul's service, a new young warrior in Israel.

The story continues with the close friendship of David and Jonathan, son of Saul. Jonathan loves David as his own soul. He gives David his robe, his armor, his sword, bow, and girdle. David is loved by women and men as well, and his popularity grows. Seeing this, Saul is angry and jealous, and he keeps a careful watch on the young hero. One day, as David plays the lyre for the brooding king, Saul throws his spear and tries to pin David to the wall. David evades him. Next, Saul makes David a commander, to remove him from his presence. But all Israel loves David, and success follows him.

Saul decides to give David one of his daughters in marriage, the daughter Merab, but at the last minute Saul changes his mind. He then hears that his daughter Michal loves David, and he begins to busily plot: he has the servants convince David that he is highly favored, and wishes him to be his son-in-law. He then asks for a marriage present of one hundred foreskins of the Philistines. Saul, hoping for David's death, is foiled when David returns victorious, with twice the number of foreskins.

> And Saul gave him his daughter Michal for a wife. But when Saul saw and knew that the Lord was with David, and that all Israel loved him, Saul was still more afraid of David.
>
> (I Samuel 18:27–29)

By this time, Saul is frenzied. He seeks to kill David, but is dissuaded by his son Jonathan. The "evil spirit," however, still hovers with Saul, and he continues to plot against his new son-in-law. Messengers go to David's house to kill him in the morning, but Michal lets David down through the window. She then takes an image, lays it on the bed, puts a pillow of goats' hair at its head, and covers it with clothes. When the messengers arrive, she tells them David is ill. The messengers go to the bed and find the image. Saul is incensed when he hears, and accuses Michal; Michal, in turn, claims David would have killed her had she not let him go.

David flees to Nob, where Abimelech the priest meets him with trembling; he gives David the holy bread to eat, and also gives him Goliath's sword. David escapes further to Achish, the king of Gath, where he pretends madness for his safety. He finally ends his flight in the cave of Adulam, and gathers about him men of ill-repute: debtors, discontents, and the distressed. David becomes their leader. Hearing the news, Saul sends out a warning: no one is to conspire with the son of Jesse. The king puts to death Abimelech and all the priests of Nob, and destroys the city. One of the priests of the Lord escapes to tell David.

Saul pursues, David escapes, and the chase continues. Near Wildgoats' Rocks Saul goes into a cave to rest. Unknown to the king, David and his men are hiding in the depths of the cave. David's friends urge him to kill Saul: David stealthily cuts off the skirt of Saul's robe, but does not attack the king. Saul, ignorant of the presence of his foe, leaves the cave, and David calls out "My Lord the king!" They speak quietly with one another, David swearing allegiance and calling Saul father. Saul weeps. They part: Saul to his home, David to his stronghold.

About this time another woman enters David's life: Abigail, wife of Nabal. Nabal is wealthy in sheep and goats, but is churlish and ill-behaved. Abigail, on the other hand, is understanding and beautiful. As Nabal shears his sheep in Carmel one day, messengers from David come to him and ask for food. The messengers explain that David's men have helped Nabal's shepherds protect their herds in the wilderness. Nabal rails at them:

> Who is David? Who is the son of Jesse? There are many servants nowadays who are breaking away from their masters. Shall I take my bread and my water and my meat that I have killed for my shearers, and give it to men who come from I do not know where? (I Samuel 25:10, 11)

When the messengers report to David, his response is brief: "Every man gird on his sword!"

Hearing of the trouble, Abigail hastens to prepare loaves, wine, sheep, grain, raisins, and figs. She ladens the asses and sends them ahead, but she does not tell her husband. David and Abigail meet near a mountain, and Abigail falls on her face before the young warrior: she pleads for her household, and rebukes Nabal for his insolence:

> Let not my lord regard this ill-natured fellow, Nabal; for as his name is, so is he; Nabal is his name, and folly is with him; but I your handmaid did not see the young men of my lord, whom you sent. (I Samuel 25:25)

David pardons her, and sends her on her way home, after receiving her gifts of food. Abigail returns home to find Nabal feasting, and very drunk. The next morning she tells him her story, and "his heart dies within him"; ten days later he is dead.

David rejoices over the death of Nabal and wastes no time: he sends messages to Abigail, asking her to be his wife. Abigail responds in kind: she makes haste, gathers her women, mounts her ass, and goes off to David. The story further reports that David has also taken Ahinoam and Jezreel for wives. Michal, David's first wife, is mentioned after a long silence; Saul has given her to a man named Palti. We hear no more of Abigail, other than a mention of a son, but we do hear more of Michal, as the story progresses.

David and Saul continue to spar with one another, and there is no final reconciliation. When Saul and Jonathan die at Mt. Gilboa, defeated by the Philistines, David is not present. He hears of the deaths from a messenger who purports to have killed Saul himself; the messenger also brings Saul's crown to David. Grieved and angry, David has the messenger killed, and then laments his loss:

> Saul and Jonathan, beloved and
> lovely!
> In life and in death they were not
> divided;
> they were swifter than eagles,
> they were stronger than lions.
> (II Samuel 1:23)

The kingdom is now divided: David is anointed king of Judah in the south, and Ishbosheth, a son of Saul, is king of Israel in the north. The house of David grows stronger, as the house of Saul grows weaker. In the house of Saul, a man named Abner quarrels with Ishbosheth over Rizpah, a former concubine of Saul's. Abner is angry and decides to change his allegiance to David, in the south. As Abner is an uncle of Saul's, David is willing to negotiate with him. He says he will make a covenant with Abner, but with one stipulation: Michal must be returned to him. A brief description of the bargain follows:

> Then David sent messengers to Ishbosheth Saul's son, saying, "Give me my wife Michal, whom I bethrothed at the price of a hundred foreskins of the Philistines." And Ishbosheth sent, and took her from her husband Palti-el the son of Laish. But her husband went with her, weeping after her all the way to Bahurim. Then Abner said to him, "Go, return;" and he returned.
> (II Samuel 3:14–16)

Once she enters the story again, Michal immediately disappears. The court intrigue heightens: Abner comes into power, but Joab, David's general, kills Abner for lack of trust and previous quarrels. Ishbosheth is also slain, and his head brought to David. David is not pleased with these continual warrings, and still mourns the loss of Saul.

The kingdom finally pulls together: Judah and Israel form a reunited country, with David as king over all. After a battle with the Jebusites, Jerusalem becomes the capital city. David takes more concubines and wives from Jerusalem, and his sons and daughters multiply.

We next hear of Michal when the ark is brought to Jerusalem. Hoping to establish his new capital as a religious center, David and thousands of others set out on a pilgrimage to reclaim the ark of God and bring it to rest. They locate the ark in northern country, place it on a new cart, and begin a jubilant journey home.

> And David and all the house of Israel were making merry before the Lord with all their might, with songs and lyres and harps and tambourines and castanets and cymbals. (II Samuel 6:5)

The ark and entire company reach Jerusalem, now called the city of David, and David, the new king, "dances before the Lord with all his might." The story notes he is clothed only with a linen ephod, that is, a light ceremonial garment covering only the front of the body—an apron of sorts.

As the ark rolls into the city, horns and shouts follow the procession. Saul's daughter Michal hears the commotion and leans out a window: she sees the king, her husband, leaping and dancing, and she despises him in her heart. The ark is set in its place, and David returns to bless his household. Michal comes to meet him, saying:

> How the king of Israel honored himself today, uncovering himself today before the eyes of his servants' maids, as one of the vulgar fellows shamelessly uncovers himself! (II Samuel 6:20b)

David justifies his behavior by saying he was "making merry before the Lord." And the Lord, says David, chose me above your father and all his house. And beyond this, he adds, the maids shall hold me in great honor. The story ends with the parting comment: "And Michal the daughter of Saul had no child to the day of her death." We hear no more of David's first wife.

Michal's dislike for David clearly shows in the final recorded incident: her dislike may have stemmed from being taken from Palti, from her family's misfortunes, or from her being one among many of David's wives. According to several countings, we can surmise that the king had at least twenty harem women and wives. Large harems were rather customary, and these supposedly increased the prestige of the ruling man. Michal's situation is especially poignant in that she is the daughter of a king, yet she is seemingly no more or less distinct than other court women. The whims of two kings hold rule over her life: first Saul uses her for political purposes, hoping for David's death, then Saul gives her to another man while she is yet married, and lastly, to strengthen his southern kingdom politically, David demands her return from Abner, after Saul's death. It is little wonder that Michal's life takes a bitter turn. In the end she is left with the worst disgrace: dying with no children to count her own.

Abigail's story, on the other hand, is refreshing. She breaks social codes, and does mostly as she pleases. One would suspect she was the true household manager, for no one objects when she packs up a large quantity of food and rides to meet a young stranger. Having lived with an irascible man for several years, she is not about to have her household razed under her for Nabal's lack of sense. Abigail herself seems to have a good, quick sense, and when opportunity comes to escape the ordinary, she loses no time in saddling her ass to become David's wife. She leaves behind both the proper period for mourning and a very wealthy household. Here is a woman who enjoys ordering her own life.

Reading

I Samuel 16 (Samuel anointing David)
17 (David and Goliath)
18 (David and Michal)
19 (David's escape)
21, 22, 24 (Saul and David)
25 (David, Abigail, and Nabal)
II Samuel 1 (David's lament)
2:1–11 (Judah and Israel)
3 (David, Abner, Michal)
4, 5 (Joab, Ishbosheth, Jerusalem)
6 (return of the ark; Michal)

Bathsheba

It happened, late one afternoon, when David arose from his

> couch and was walking upon the roof of the king's house, that he saw from the roof a woman bathing; and the woman was very beautiful. (II Samuel 11:2)

King David busies himself with affairs of state: he wars with the Philistines and various other powers, and is victorious. The story speaks of his fame:

> And David won a name for himself . . . . So David reigned over all Israel; and David administered justice and equality to all his people. (II Samuel 8:13, 15)

About this time, in the spring of a particular year, David sends his general Joab into battle, but he remains at Jerusalem. One afternoon, as he walks on the roof, he sees, on another roof, a woman bathing. The woman is quite beautiful. David sends to learn of the woman; he finds that she is Bathsheba, the daughter of Eliam, the wife of Uriah the Hittite. Without delay, David sends messengers to take Bathsheba: e comes to him and "he lay with her." The story adds, in parenthesis, that Bathsheba is purifying herself from her uncleanness. She returns home, finds in time that she has conceived, and sends a message to David, saying she is with child.

Upon receiving her word, David then sends to Joab, his general, asking for Uriah the Hittite. Uriah has been in battle all this time. When Uriah comes into the king's presence, David makes small talk: how is Joab? he asks; how are the people faring, and how does the war prosper? He then sends Uriah home: "Go down to your house, and wash your feet." A present from the king follows. But Uriah sleeps at the door of the king's house, and does not return home. David hears of this and questions Uriah. Uriah replies:

> The ark and Israel and Judah dwell in booths; and my lord Joab and the servants of my lord are camping in the open field; shall I then go to my house, to eat and drink, and to lie with my wife? As you live, and as your soul lives, I will not do this thing.
> (II Samuel 11:11)

David's next ploy, as Uriah remains loyal, is to invite Uriah to eat and drink with him one evening. Uriah becomes drunk, but still he does not go to Bathsheba. The next morning David writes a letter to Joab, which Uriah carries to the general:

> Set Uriah in the forefront of the hardest fighting, and then draw back from him, that he may be struck down, and die.
> (II Samuel 11:15)

Joab does as he is instructed, and in due course, Uriah dies in battle. When David hears the news he sends back to Joab: "Do not let this matter trouble you, for the sword devours now one and now another . . . ." Bathsheba, also hearing of Uriah's death, makes lamentation for her husband. After the period of mourning is over, David sends and brings her to his house: Bathsheba becomes his wife, and she bears a son. But the thing which David has done displeases the Lord.

We now hear of Nathan the prophet, a successor of Samuel. Nathan rebukes David through the telling of a parable: "there were two men in a city, one rich and one poor. The rich man had many flocks and herds, but the poor man had only one small ewe lamb. The ewe ate and drank with him and his children; she was like a daughter. But one day a traveler came to the rich man, seeking food. The rich man, rather than take one of his own flock, took the poor man's lamb instead, and killed it."

David hears Nathan's parable, and is angry: the man who has done this deserves to die! he says. Nathan turns to David and says: "You are the man." For the death of Uriah the Hittite, and for the taking of Bathsheba, the Lord is very angry. David says to Nathan: "I have sinned against the Lord." Nathan says that the Lord has put away his sin, has forgiven David, but nevertheless the child who is born will die.

Then, says the story, the Lord strikes the child of Bathsheba and David, and the child is ill. David prays to God and fasts, and lies all night upon the ground. On the seventh day of the illness the child dies. David rises from the earth, washes, changes clothes, and worships. Then he eats, and later goes to Bathsheba:

> Then David comforted his wife, Bathsheba, and went into to her, and lay with her; and she bore a son, and he called his name Solomon. And the Lord loved him . . . . (II Samuel 12:24)

During the years of Solomon's youth there is no record of Bathsheba, but when David is old and dying, we hear of her again. The story describes King David as being advanced in years: he is covered with clothes, but cannot get warm. The servants find a beautiful young maiden named Abishag to be David's nurse and comfort. Abishag lies next to David to keep him warm, but the old king does not "know" her, in the sexual sense. David's son Adonijah, seeing his father's fraility, mutinies for the throne. Joab the general follows Adonijah, but Nathan the prophet does not.

Nathan warns Bathsheba: have you not heard, he says, that Adonijah is king, and David does not know it? He then counsels Bathsheba, telling her to plead with David for the reign of Solomon. She goes to the king's chambers and makes her request.

> My lord, you swore to your maidservant by the Lord your God, saying, "Solomon your son shall reign after me, and he shall sit upon my throne." And now, behold, Adonijah is king, although you, my lord the king, do not know it. (I Kings 1:17, 18)

Nathan makes a timely entrance, and confirms Bathsheba's words. They tell the king of the feasting and drinking going on with Adonijah and his followers. David responds quickly: he proclaims Solomon king, and gives instructions that he is to be anointed king over Israel. So it is done, and Solomon reigns. David dies soon after. We hear of Bathsheba in one more instance, when she asks a favor of King Solomon. After this, she is not again mentioned.

Bathsheba's story is intriguing in that she is so often characterized as temptress, seducer, and adulterer; even the narrator subtly emphasizes this by indirectly refering to her as "unclean." When she first meets the king she is purifying herself from her menstruation, and the writer makes it a point to mention this. One male commentator describes her character as a "dirty, apologetic gray."[2]

As Bathsheba does not seem to fit the wicked woman image, we would hold these descriptions in question. In the David-Bathsheba-Uriah story, David is clearly the villain. Nathan pointedly shows this in his parable. Uriah is the hero, an honorable man wishing to serve his lord. Bathsheba remains the victim, the little ewe lamb, in the sense that she ostensibly has no choice in the matter: a king commands, and she must obey. King David is often considered a hero, yet in this story he calls for a married woman, tries to pass her pregnancy off on her husband, reduces the husband to drunkenness, and, in desperation, finally has him killed. It is to his credit that he honors the woman by marrying her, and caring for her child.

By now David has many wives, including all of King Saul's harem, and in the end, Bathsheba apparently is highly favored. She is listened to by the aging king, and her request is honored. Nathan the prophet remains her ally, although for his own political purposes, and Solomon reigns as king. We prefer to see Bathsheba characterized as a caring companion and mother, one who lives to enjoy the reign of her son.

Reading
II Samuel 11, 12
I Kings 1
2:13–27

Tamar

> Now Absalom, David's son, had a beautiful sister, whose name was Tamar; and after a time Amnon, David's son, loved her.
> (II Samuel 13:1)

In continuing the story of Bathsheba we have moved ahead in time, so now we return to earlier days. David still lives, Solomon has been born, and the story picks up with the tale of Tamar and her brothers.

David's son Absalom has a beautiful sister named Tamar. Another son, Amnon, loves Tamar: he is so tormented over this passion that he makes himself ill. Tamar, we are told, is yet a virgin. Tamar is in actuality a full sister of Absalom, and a half-sister of Amnon. Amnon is the king's eldest son, and therefore successor to the throne; Absalom is next in line. The story opens with a conversation between Amnon and his friend Jonadab, "a very crafty man":

> O son of the king, why are you so haggard morning after morning? Will you not tell me? (II Samuel 13:4a)

Amnon confesses loving his sister Tamar, and Jonadab gives advice: lie down on your bed, he says, and pretend to be ill. When your father comes to see you, ask for your sister Tamar, that she might come and prepare food for you.

Amnon does as Jonadab bids, and all goes according to plan. He requests that Tamar "make a couple of cakes in my sight" that he might eat from her hand. David the king sends for Tamar, and she goes to her brother Amnon's house. She takes dough, kneads it, makes cakes, and bakes them. Then she empties the pans before Amnon, but he refuses to eat. After sending the remaining servants away, Amnon then tells Tamar to bring the food into his private chamber, that he might eat from her hand. This she does, and as she draws near to him, he takes hold of her and says: "Come, lie with me, my sister." Tamar answers:

> No, my brother, do not force me; for such a thing is not done in Israel; do not do this wanton folly. As for me, where could I carry my shame? (II Samuel 13:12, 13)

Tamar tries to convince Amnon of his foolishness; she asks him to speak with the king, for permission to marry. But Amnon pays her no heed, and, being the stronger, he forces her and lies with her. The tone of the story suddenly shifts: Amnon now hates Tamar with a very great hatred. He tells her to arise and be gone. She refuses, saying that sending her away is even a greater wrong. But again Amnon will not listen to her. He calls the young man who serves him and commands him to "put this woman out of my presence, and bolt the door after her." The servant does as he is told, bolting the door after Tamar:

> Now she was wearing a long robe with sleeves; for thus were the virgin daughters of the king clad of old . . . . And Tamar put ashes on her head, and rent the long robe which she wore; and she laid her hand on her head, and went away, crying aloud as she went. (II Samuel 13:18a, 19)

When Tamar returns home she is met by her brother Absalom, who asks if she has been with Amnon. Hold your peace, my sister, he says, for Amnon is your brother. And he further adds: do not take this to heart. Tamar then dwells, a desolate woman, in Absalom's house. When the king hears of the happenings, he is very angry. But Absalom "spoke to Amnon neither good nor bad," for Absalom now hates Amnon, because he has forced his sister Tamar.

Two years go by. It is the time of sheepshearing, and Absalom invites all the king's sons to festivities. The king, unable to attend, gives Absalom his blessing and sends along Amnon, whose presence Absalom has especially requested. In the meantime, Absalom has instructed his servants:

> Mark when Amnon's heart is merry with wine, and when I say to you, "Strike Amnon," then kill him. (II Samuel 13:28a)

During the festivities the servants strike Amnon dead, and all the other sons mount their mules and flee. A rumor reaches David that all his sons have been slain, and he tears his garments and lays on the earth. But Jonadab brings the truth: Amnon alone is dead. Absalom long ago determined this from the day Tamar was forced, he says.

So Absalom flees and goes to Gesher, where he stays for three years. We are told the king mourns for his son day after day, and his spirit "longs to go forth to Absalom." After Absalom avenges his sister Tamar, we hear no more of the king's daughter, and the small story comes to a close.

Once again we encounter a woman whose story is bound with political overtones. As in the case of Dinah's rape, Tamar's rape becomes an incentive for revenge. Amnon, the king's eldest son, would have been king. Absalom was next in succession. And if we read the story further, we see that Absalom rises in revolt against his father David, and is later killed by Joab. Early on, then, Absalom has intentions of capturing the throne, and he therefore makes good use of the Tamar-Amnon incident. The question remains: who is there to care for Tamar? Amnon rapes her, Absalom tells her "not to take this to heart," and the king does nothing to find Tamar a suitable husband. It is of little concern, it seems, that she would never marry or bear children, and she remains a despairing woman. For the daughter of a king to be humiliated would be a lifelong shame. We are left with a haunting and poignant portrait of Tamar: ashes on her head, long robe torn, wailing as she goes.

Reading
II Samuel 13

Rizpah

> Then Rizpah the daughter of Aiah took sackcloth, and spread it for herself on the rock, from the beginning of the harvest until rain fell upon them from the heavens; and she did not allow the birds of the air to come upon them by day, or the beasts of the field by night. (II Samuel 21:10)

Before we leave the telling of the reign of David, we might consider one small story tucked away near the end of II Samuel. The woman Rizpah has been mentioned once earlier, as a concubine of Saul's. After Saul's death, she traditionally belonged in the new king's harem, in this case, Ishbosheth's. But Abner, Saul's uncle, also laid claim to her, and this disagreement was the cause of Abner's defection to David's side. The next we hear of Rizpah, her two sons, born to Saul, have been hanged by the Gibeonites, at David's request. Several things occur before we are brought to this point in the story.

After the story of Tamar, we hear the account of Absalom's conspiracy against David. Absalom returns to Jerusalem and secretly begins to build forces against the king, although the king favors him. The rebellion begins, and David is forced to flee Jerusalem. Much intrigue and battle follows, and David's army defeats Absalom's. David orders Joab to "deal gently for my sake with the young man Absalom," but Joab instead kills Absalom while he hangs caught in a tree. David is deeply moved, and mourns his son:

> O my son Absalom, my son, my son Absalom! Would I had died instead of you, O Absalom, my son, my son! (II Samuel 18:33b)

David returns to Jerusalem, and a new revolt occurs; there is more murder and bloodshed, and Joab quells the rebellion. The story now changes, referring back to an earlier time, and we are told that there has been a famine in the land for three years. David seeks "the face of the Lord" for direction. God tells David there is "bloodguilt on Saul and on his house" for putting the Gibeonites to death. David calls the Gibeonites, to confer with them. What shall I do for you, he asks; how shall I make expiation? The Gibeonites reply that it is not a matter of silver or gold; they then ask for the death of seven of Saul's sons "that we may hang them up before the Lord at Gibeon on the mountain of the Lord." So David gives up seven of Saul's sons: two sons of Rizpah, and five of Saul's grandsons. The Gibeonites hang them on the mountain, before the Lord. The barley harvest has just begun.

Rizpah, the daughter of Aiah, takes sackcloth and spreads it for herself on a rock, near the bodies of her sons. And there she stays, from the beginning of the harvest in the spring, until rain falls in late autumn. During the day she shields her sons from the birds, and protects them from beasts by night. David hears of Rizpah's long vigil, and he goes to collect the bones of Saul and his son Jonathan. Gathering their bones, and the bones of seven sons hanged, he then buries them with honor in the tomb of Kish, Saul's father. The rains have come, and the expiation is completed. Rizpah, we can imagine, goes home, knowing her sons now rest.

Rizpah's story, though brief, is one to capture the heart. She is, in a sense, representative of many Old Testament women, for she has few rights. Her sons are trapped in political retribution, and she has no recourse. Yet her suffering and her patient waiting do not go unseen. Sons of the king have been dishonored. Not only were they hanged unnecessarily, in her eyes, but they were also left to winds and prey—an added disgrace. But Rizpah keeps vigil over long months of sun and rain, and her steadfast love, in the end, prevails. She lives to see her sons recognized, and with this we hear no more.

The great period of Saul and David now draws to a close: Saul is dead, David is soon to die, and Solomon reigns. The strength of the united kingdom of Israel begins to wane, and we come upon less heroic, more troubled times for the people of God.

Reading

II Samuel 3:6–11 (Abner, Rizpah, Ishbosheth)
II Samuel 21:1–14 (Rizpah and David)

FIVE

Women of Prophets' Times

1. Queen of Israel and wife of Ahab; fierce foe of Elijah the prophet, and worshipper of the Goddess. **2.** Poor widow whose son is raised to life by Elijah. **3.** Wealthy woman and patron of Elisha, whose son is restored to life by the prophet. **4.** Queen of Judah, of the family of Ahab. Destroys the royal family after her son's death. **5.** Woman prophet who interprets lost scroll of Deuteronomy for king Josiah, and thus begins reform.

With the defeat of Adonijah, David's son, and with the anointing of Solomon, a new time has begun. Before David dies, he warns Solomon of several enemies, and they are all purged from the new kingdom. Adonijah and Joab are killed, and their followers exiled or slain. Solomon, now in complete command, marries Pharoah's daughter, who comes to Jerusalem from Egypt, and a political alliance is established.

Solomon, says the story, loves the Lord. The Lord appears to Solomon in a dream, telling Solomon to ask for whatever he wills. Solomon asks for wisdom:

> Give thy servant therefore an understanding mind to govern thy people, that I may discern between good and evil; for who is able to govern this thy great people? (I Kings 3:9)

God is pleased with the request, and grants Solomon his wish, granting him also riches and honor. We next hear a small story of Solomon and two women, in which he exercises his new wisdom.

Two harlots come to the king and stand before him. One woman tells the story: both women gave birth to children, just three days apart, and in the same house. Both had sons, but one died in the night. The woman whose son died rose at midnight and switched sons, while the other woman lay sleeping. Fierce arguments followed between the women once the deed was discovered; they have now come to Solomon to settle the matter. In response, Solomon calls for a sword and tells the women to "divide the living child in two, and give half to the one, and half to the other." One mother tells Solomon to give the child to the other woman, rather than kill it, while the other woman says to divide it in half. Solomon discerns the true mother, and all of Israel praises his judgment.

The kingdom continues to grow in wisdom and wealth. Solomon organizes his domain, and sends for cedars of Lebanon, and cypress timber, to build a temple for the Lord. In seven years the temple is completed, and in thirteen years Solomon builds for himself a palace. After the building of the house of the Lord and the king's house, God appears to Solomon for a second time:

> I have heard your prayer and your supplication, which you have made before me; I have consecrated this house which you have built, and put my name there forever; my eyes and my heart will be there for all time. (I Kings 9:3)

The Lord instructs Solomon to "walk before me, as David your father walked," for if Solomon turns aside, warns the Lord, Israel will be cut off from the land. And further: Israel will become a proverb, the house of the Lord will become a heap of ruins, if the people forsake the Lord their God.

With this solemn warning, the story continues. The Queen of Sheba, from the land of Arabia, pays Solomon a visit. She arrives in splendor, accompanied by camels, spices, gold, and precious stones. Having heard of Solomon's fame, she plies him with questions: Solomon withstands her questioning, and the queen is duly impressed with his wisdom, his house, his food, clothing, and burnt offerings. She praises him for his abundance and for his Lord, and gives him gifts of gold and spices and stones. Solomon rejoins with gifts of his own, and king and queen part amicably. Traders and merchants also pay Solomon their respects, and in time, the king amasses great wealth. Thus King Solomon excells all the kings of the earth in riches and wisdom. The whole earth seeks his great wisdom, and presents him with silver, gold, garments, myrrh, spices, horses, and mules, year after year.

We now begin to hear a darker side: the story reports that Solomon loves many foreign women, especially those forbidden in marriage by the Lord.

> . . . Solomon clung to these in love. He had seven hundred wives, princesses, and three hundred concubines; and his wives turned away his heart . . . after other gods; and his heart was not wholly true to the Lord his God . . . . (I Kings 11:2c, 3, 4)

So Solomon does what is evil in the sight of the Lord, and the Lord is angry. God warns Solomon that if he is not faithful, his kingdom will be torn from him, and divided in parts. Adversaries begin to rise up against Solomon: Hadad, Rezon, and Jeroboam. A prophet named Ahijah speaks also of division to come, and of the rule of Jeroboam. Solomon attempts to kill Jeroboam, but Jeroboam finds safety in Egypt until Solomon's death. Some time later Solomon dies, leaving his son Rehoboam to reign.

Rehoboam is a worse taskmaster than his father: he refuses counsel of the old men, and uses stinging whips on the people. Jeroboam, now a present threat, quarrels with the new king, and the kingdom revolts and divides: Rehoboam to Judah and the south; Jeroboam to Israel and the north.

> What portion have we in David?
> We have no inheritance in the son
> of Jesse.
> To your tents, O Israel!
> Look now to your own house,
> David.
>
> (I Kings 12:16)

And this begins years of division, turbulence, and political skirmishings.

Rehoboam and Jeroboam are succeeded by their sons, who in turn war with one another and raise up other minor kings who die or are murdered. On occasion the people take the rule in their own hands, and many now worship foreign gods. Dissolution reigns, and the once united military kingdom, strongly forged by Saul and David, remains fragmented. Into these times come three striking figures: Ahab, Jezebel, and Elijah.

Jezebel

> Ahab told Jezebel all that Elijah had done, and how he had slain all the prophets with the sword. Then Jezebel sent a messenger to Elijah, saying, "So may the gods do to me, and more also, if I do not make your life as the life of one of them by this time tomorrow." (I Kings 19:1, 2)

Ahab reigns as king in the north, after his father Omri. Omri did much evil, and Ahab does even more. Ahab takes for his wife a foreign woman called Jezebel; Ahab and Jezebel serve Baal, the fertility god of Canaan, and Asherah, a mother-goddess and fertility deity. They erect an altar to Baal and set up an image of the Asherah. God, the story says, is exceedingly provoked.

Elijah the Tishbite, an unintroduced man, comes to Ahab, and speaks:

> As the Lord the God of Israel lives, before whom I stand, there shall be neither dew nor rain these years, except by my word.
> (I Kings 17:1)

God then speaks with Elijah, telling him to "hide himself by the brook Cherith": go into the desert land east of the Jordan. Elijah goes, and there he is cared for by the ravens who bring him bread and meat, mornings and evenings. While the water lasts, Elijah drinks from a brook. The water then dries up, and there is no rain.

Elijah is determined to prove that the God of Israel controls the rain, as the Canaanite god Baal has been credited this work from his followers. After three years in the desert, then, God sends Elijah back to Ahab, with the message that rain will soon follow. Jezebel, in the meantime, has "cut off" the prophets of the Lord, but Obadiah, a follower of the Lord, has hid a hundred prophets in a cave. Obadiah and Elijah meet as the prophet returns home, and Ahab, upon hearing the news, comes to meet Elijah.

"Is it you, you troubler of Israel?" Ahab asks, and Elijah replies that

Ahab is the faulty one, as he has forsaken the Lord for Baal. They decide on a test: Elijah calls for the prophets of Asherah the goddess and Baal the god to gather with him and all of Israel, on Mount Carmel. The contest begins: both sides place a sacrificed bull on wood, and proceed to call on deities to bring fire. For hours the prophets of Baal limp and rave about the altar, but nothing happens. Elijah then calls on the God of Israel, and fire consumes the offering. The people fall on their faces:

> The Lord, he is God; the Lord, he is God. (I Kings 18:39)

They seize the prophets of Baal, and kill them. And then the rain comes, ending the famine.

Ahab returns to tell Jezebel of the happenings, and she is incensed. She sends a message to Elijah, saying she will avenge her gods with his death. Afraid, Elijah quickly departs for the wilderness, where angels give him cakes baked on hot stones, and jars of water. He then travels, refreshed, to Horeb the mount of God. Here Elijah meets the Lord: "a still small voice" instructs him to anoint Elisha to be prophet in his place.

Ahab, in the meantime, wars with Syria. He appears now to be a popular ruler; the people encourage him and the prophets of the Lord support him. But victory is short-lived: Elijah soon returns to denounce Ahab and Jezebel for the incident of Naboth's vineyard. Ahab is pleased with the vineyard of Naboth, and asks that he might have it for a vegetable garden. Naboth refuses. Vexed and sullen, Ahab returns to his house, lays down on his bed, and eats no food. Jezebel questions him: "Why is your spirit so vexed that you eat no food?" He tells her the story, and she replies:

> Do you now govern Israel? Arise, and eat bread, and let your heart be cheerful; I will give you the vineyard of Naboth . . . .
> (I Kings 21:7)

As good as her word, Jezebel gains the property: she has Naboth stoned to death. Hearing the news, Elijah goes to meet Ahab. Have you found me, O my enemy? asks Ahab, and Elijah answers that Ahab will receive evil for evil: his family will be utterly swept away, eaten by dogs and birds. Some time later Ahab is killed in battle, and his sons do indeed inherit the curse. Several years after Ahab's death, Jezebel is killed in a political warring. She is thrown out a window by her own servants, and horses trample her in the street.

The story of Jezebel, Ahab, Elijah, and their various gods is one of intrigue, power, violence, and fear. For centuries Jezebel has been labeled evil, her very name a synonym for wickedness. Says Edith Deen:

> In her evil power over her husband, Jezebel might be compared to Shakespeare's Lady Macbeth. In her fanaticism, she might be likened to Mary, Queen of Scots. Her death, though far more bitter and bloody, suggests the death on the guillotine of another alien queen, Marie Antoinette. And like Catherine de Medici, Jezebel is remembered as an outstanding example of what a woman ought not to be.[1]

While we cannot claim Jezebel to be without fault, we can at least credit her for being the daughter, wife, and mother of kings, and perhaps not as barbarous as she often appears. And we can also raise some curious questions: what makes her so alien? What makes her so feared? Wherein lies her power?

To begin, Jezebel was a follower of Asherah, the Canaanite fertility Goddess. This fact alone causes her to be scorned by the writer, as in the mind of Israel, Yahweh alone was God; all other gods were impostors, pretenders, and to be purged. Rosemary Ruether comments:

> Old Testament religion is traditionally presented to us as an uncompromising war against nature religion . . . . The Old Testament rejection of female symbols for God, and perhaps also of female religious leaders, probably had something to do with this struggle against Canaanite religion, with its powerful goddess figures and its female-dominated ceremonies of worship.[2]

And Merlin Stone, author of *When God Was a Woman*, dates worship of the Great Goddess as far back as 25,000 B.C., while Abraham is believed to have lived no earlier than 1800 B.C.[3] The Goddess was most ancient and highly revered, while the deity Yahweh appeared as a relative youngster on the religious scene.

According to the Jezebel-Ahab story, four hundred prophets of Asherah and four hundred fifty prophets of Baal ate at Jezebel's table. These, then, would represent formidable rivals to Yahweh of Israel.

It will be noted, says one source, that every Old Testament mention of Asherah (some forty times) is a condemnation of her, or an approval of those who tried to destroy her cult. The necessity for these reforms makes it highly likely that the worship of Asherah was quite popular in ancient Israel.[4]

Jezebel, then, is to be feared, for she is a powerful force with a strong following. The writer of the narrative would naturally wish to cast her in a disparaging light, for her very presence threatens the heart of Israel. This is not to say Jezebel's character is sterling, for she is as political and as ruthless as the next, but it is to call into question the basis for her condemnation. Female symbols for God, female Goddesses, and female rulers appear to evoke deep-seated resistance in the minds of some, and it is this which needs to be examined.

Reading

I Kings 1–15 (David's death; Solomon's reign; the divided kingdom)
I Kings 16, 17 (Ahab, Jezebel, Elijah)
18, 19 (Mount Carmel: Baal and Yahweh; Mount Horeb)
21 (Naboth's vineyard)
I Kings 22:37 (Ahab's death)
II Kings 9:30–37 (Jezebel's death)

Widow of Zarephath and Shunammite Woman

> So Elijah arose and went to Zarephath; and when he came to the gate of the city, behold, a widow was there gathering sticks . . . .
> (I Kings 17:10)

> One day Elisha went on to Shunem, where a wealthy woman lived, who urged him to eat some food. (II Kings 4:8a)

Two small tales of women appear within the Elijah-Elisha stories, and we should not pass through without their mention. The first appears before the great contest on Mount Carmel. Elijah is commanded by the Lord to go to Zarephath, on the Phoenician coast. When he reaches the gate he sees a widow gathering sticks, and asks her to bring him some water. As the woman turns to fetch the water, Elijah calls to her again: "Bring me a morsel of bread in your hand." She replies that she has nothing baked, only a handful of meal in a jar and a little oil. And now, she says, she is gathering sticks to make a meal for herself and her son, and then they will die. Elijah reassures her: fear not, he says, make me a little cake anyway, and afterwards feed yourself and your son. The meal and the oil miraculously multiply, and Elijah stays with the woman many days.

After a time the woman's son becomes quite ill, so ill that there is "no breath left in him." Distraught, the widow upbraids Elijah for being the cause of her troubles:

> What have you against me, O man of God? You have come to me to bring my sin to remembrance, and to cause the death of my son! (I Kings 17:18)

Elijah carries her son to an upper chamber, lays him upon a bed, and prays to the Lord. He then stretches himself upon the child three times, and the child revives. He returns the boy to his mother, and she responds:

> Now I know that you are a man of God, and that the word of the Lord in your mouth is truth. (I Kings 17:24)

The second tale involves the successor of Elijah, Elisha. By now Elijah has been taken to heaven by a whirlwind, with a chariot and horses of fire. His mantle falls to Elisha, who in turn receives the spirit of the Lord. He proceeds with a series of miracles: at Jericho he cures a spring of water; at Bethel he curses small boys who jeer at him, calling him "baldhead," and they are eaten by she-bears. He later meets a poor widow whose sons are about to be sold into slavery by a creditor, but Elisha causes her oil jars to be filled, and the sons are saved and debts paid.

Following this last miracle is the story of the Shunammite woman. Elisha goes to Shunem, the home of a wealthy woman who gives him food whenever he passes by. Wishing to care for Elisha, the woman talks her husband into housing the "holy man of God" in his own private chamber. One day as he rests, Elisha calls the woman into his presence and asks, through his servant Gehazi, what can be done for her. She does not reply directly, but the servant suggests: "Well, she has no son, and her husband is old." Elisha tells her she shall bear a son the next spring season, and so she does. The child grows, and goes out one day among the reapers. At once his head begins to ache from the heat of the sun, and he later dies in his mother's lap. She lays him on the prophet's bed, and goes in haste to find Elisha. Elisha, seeing her approach, sends his servant to inquire after the family's well-being:

> Look, yonder is the Shunammite; run at once to meet her, and say to her, Is it well with you? Is it well with your husband? Is it well with the child? And she answered, It is well.
>
> (II Kings 4:25b–26)

The woman then approaches Elisha and catches hold of his feet. The servant tries to push her away, but Elisha sees her distress. He immediately dispatches Gehazi to the child, telling him to lay the prophet's staff upon the boy's face. The Shunammite woman refuses to leave Elisha; he finally relents and begins to follow the woman to her child. Gehazi, in the meantime, reaches the son, but the magic of the staff fails; the servant turns back to meet the prophet: Elisha arrives at the house, prays to the Lord, stretches himself out upon the child, and the boy revives. Elisha then instructs Gehazi to "call this Shunammite." The woman comes, falls at his feet, bowing, and takes her son.

We later hear of the Shunammite woman one last time. Elisha tells the woman to depart with her household, for a famine is coming. The woman goes to the land of the Philistines for seven years, and then returns. We hear nothing of her husband during this interlude. She then appeals to the king for the restoration of her house and land, and with Elisha's help, these are returned to her.

The stories of the widow of Zarephath and the Shunammite woman, common folktales, are a sharp contrast to the Jezebel story. Both of these women exhibit a faith in the God of the prophets and are therefore acceptable in the mind of the storyteller. For their obedience and diligence they are rewarded: their sons are raised to life and all is well again. They are models of giving, receptive, faithful women, having no semblance to the portrait of the Goddess-worshipper Jezebel.

Several points in these stories give us pause. We might bring into question the prophets' associations with the women. Why does the first tale mention the woman's sins as being yoked with the death of her son, and why did the prophet choose to live with her? Further, in the second story, the servant makes a point of the old age of the woman's husband. The woman herself is quite taken with Elisha, enough to furnish him with room and board. The prophet maintains an odd association with the woman, speaking in her presence through his servant, and seeming nervous about her approach after the collapse of her son. His anxiety might account for the woman's answer of "It is well," when, in fact, it was not at all well. Possibly she might have felt it necessary to cloak the truth to gain his audience. This could be idle speculation, as we cannot interpret these stories too literally. Yet there remains an uneasiness: could the prophets have used the women for their own gains—food, shelter, companionship—to later reward them?

Reading

I Kings 17:8–24 (Widow of Zarephath)
II Kings 2,4:1–7 (ascension of Elijah; Elisha's miracles)
4:8–37 (Shunammite woman)
8:1–6 (Shunammite woman)

Athaliah

> Now when Athaliah the mother of Ahaziah saw that her son was dead, she arose and destroyed all the royal family.
> (II Kings 11:1)

We now come to Athaliah, the only queen of Israel, the daughter of Jezebel and Ahab. Ahab forms an alliance with Jehoshaphat, king of Judah, by marrying Athaliah to the king's son, Jehoram. Athaliah and Jehoram have a son, named Ahaziah.

Following the death of Ahab, the political scene begins to rapidly disintegrate: Elisha, in the northern kingdom, anoints a certain Jehu as king of Israel. Jehu is commanded by the Lord to "strike down the house of Ahab" to avenge on Jezebel the blood of the prophets and the servants of the Lord. Jehu then goes to find Joram, the present king of Israel, and Ahaziah, the king of Judah, who are visiting one another in their chariots.

> And when Joram saw Jehu, he said, "Is it peace, Jehu?" He answered, "What peace can there be, so long as the harlotries and the sorceries of your mother Jezebel are so many?" Then

> Joram reined about and fled, saying to Ahaziah, "Treachery, O Ahaziah!" (II Kings 9:22, 23)

Jehu draws his bow, shoots Joram in the back, and pursues and kills Ahaziah, Athaliah's son.

Jehu then goes to find Jezebel, and causes her to be thrown out the window and trampled. He continues the destruction, and there is a massacre of the princes of Israel and the princes of Judah.

> So Jehu slew all that remained of the house of Ahab in Jezreel, all his great men, and his familiar friends, until he left him none remaining. (II Kings 10:11)

Following this, Jehu, proclaiming "Come with me, and see my zeal for the Lord," sets a trap for all the prophets, worshippers, and priests of Baal. He utterly destroys them, demolishes the pillar of Baal, and demolishes the house of Baal, making it into a latrine. The Lord praises Jehu, saying he has "done well in carrying out what is right in my eyes, and have done to the house of Ahab according to all that was in my heart . . . ." Jehu's sons, says the Lord, will sit on the throne of Israel.

Athaliah is now introduced into this setting. When she hears of her son the king's death, she destroys all the royal family. But one small prince, Joash, is spirited away and hidden for six years. Athaliah, after eliminating any possible contenders to the throne, now reigns over the land.

Years later Joash and his following return. He is crowned, anointed, and proclaimed king: the people clap and shout. Athaliah, hearing the noise, goes to the house of the Lord. Seeing the young king and the rejoicing people, she cries "Treason! Treason!" No one comes to her aid. The captains of the army slay Athaliah and her followers in the king's house, as the priest will not let her be killed in the house of the Lord. Then all the people of the land go to the house of Baal, tear it down, break the altars and images, and kill the priest. Joash reigns, and the city is once again quiet.

The reign of Athaliah is brief, but telling. The only woman to sit on the throne of David, she generally does not receive good reviews, either from the scripture or from commentators:

> Athaliah . . . was the extreme in wickedness . . . . Evil ran in her veins.[5]

There is nothing in the story to support a favorable or admirable character for this queen, but it is surprising to see how she compares with the hero of Israel, Jehu. Jehu wins praise from the writers of the narrative who speak for the Lord, for his widespread, unrelenting massacre. His "cunning" against the worshippers of Baal is applauded, and he is rewarded with generations seated on the throne of Israel.

Athaliah, in contrast, begins and ends disfavorably. She is the granddaughter of Omri, considered an evil king, and daughter to two of scripture's prominent villains. She kills off her family, worships foreign gods, and is entirely disreputable. One begins to wonder, in all these affairs, where the truth lies. The writers of the narrative carry high their bias and intolerance, and while Athaliah is not without fault, we would wonder at the reality of the story and what possible character could be seen, viewed through another glass.

Reading

II Kings 9 (Joram, Ahaziah, Jehu, Jezebel)
10 (princes of Israel and Judah, worshippers of Baal slain)
11 (Athaliah and Joash)

Huldah

> So Hilkiah the priest, and Ahikam, and Achbor, and Shaphan, and Asaiah went to Huldah the prophetess, the wife of Shallum the son of Tikvah, son of Harhas, keeper of the wardrobe . . . and they talked with her. (II Kings 22:14)

We now come to the last of our Old Testament women to be considered: Huldah, the prophetess. Huldah is the third mentioned woman prophet, following Miriam and Deborah. All three women differed by nature and by functioning, as prophets of the Lord. Miriam was called prophet because of her ecstatic dance and song, her charisma; Deborah was widely respected because of her military prowess and counsel; Huldah as prophet again appears in the role of advisor, and as something of a spiritual guide.

Following Athaliah's death, the histories of Israel and Judah once again plunge into chaos and disorder. For a time, when Jehoash (Joash) is king in Judah, there is stability. He repairs the temple in Jerusalem and rids the land of Baal-worship. After his death, sundry kings and their sons reign in both Judah and Israel, accompanied by the usual warrings, conspiracies, assasinations, and intrigue. Samaria, Israel's center, is captured by Assyrians, and several tribes are carried into captivity. The northern kingdom comes to an end, and the story continues with the reign of Hezekiah, king of Judah in the south. Hezekiah "does what is right in the eyes of the Lord": he removes the altars, breaks pillars, and cuts down the Goddess Asherah. Assyria threatens the southern kingdom, but Judah is victorious, and the land saved. Hezekiah is then succeeded by Manasseh, considered an evil king, who is succeeded by Amnon. Following Amnon we hear of Josiah, who comes like fresh wind; he is a good king:

> And he did what was right in the eyes of the Lord, and walked in all the way of David his father, and he did not turn aside to the right hand or to the left. (II Kings 22:2)

During Josiah's reign, in the year 621 B.C., a very important book is found. This story begins when the king sends Hilkiah, the high priest, to "reckon the amount of the money . . . brought into the house of the Lord." Josiah wishes to repair the temple, and Hilkiah acts as overseer. In the course of the reconstruction Hilkiah comes across a scroll, apparently found in a collection box, or possibly in some rubbish about to be removed. Hilkiah says to Shaphan, a temple scribe: "I have found the book of the law in the house of the Lord." Shaphan reads the scroll, realizes its importance, and goes to tell the king. The king hears the words and rends his clothes, for this is the book of Deuteronomy, long lost. Go, says Josiah to several of his men, inquire of the Lord for me and for the people, concerning this book. The Lord's wrath is great, he says, for we have not obeyed the words of this book.

Hilkiah and Shaphan and three others go off to find Huldah the prophetess, who greets them:

> Thus says the Lord, the God of Israel: Tell the man who sent you to me, Thus says the Lord, Behold I will bring evil upon this place and upon its inhabitants, all the words of the book which the king of Judah has read. Because you have forsaken me . . . .
> (II Kings 22:16, 17a)

She further says that because of Josiah's repentance, he will not see the impending evil, but will be "gathered to his grave in peace." On this hearing, Josiah begins a massive reform, following the laws of the scroll: he gathers the people, reads the book, and purges the land of alien gods, goddesses, and priests. He then dies, not a peaceful death, but on the battlefield. Of Huldah we hear no more.

Huldah is something of a mysterious figure. No doubt she carried considerable weight in the religious community, for when the emergency arises and Josiah calls for immediate translation of the lost scroll, Huldah is consulted at once. We know nothing of her except that she is a prophet, she is married to a man who keeps the king's wardrobe, and she lives in the Second Quarter of Jerusalem, within walking distance of the temple. She seems to be something of a seer: a woman of wisdom, a guide, one who receives missives directly from the Lord. She is not counselor as much as oracle, and her words are heard with highest respect. Woman as prophet now appears to be a stationary figure, one accepted by the community and one whose wisdom is sought.

Reading

II Kings 12–17 (Jehoash; warfare; Assyrian captivity)
18–21 (Hezekiah and successors)
22 (Josiah, Hilkiah, Huldah)
23 (Josiah's reforms)

With Huldah's words we close the stories of the women of Israel, from Genesis through II Kings. In actuality, there are no further women to be accounted for, save Ruth and Esther, whose stories were written much later, and who do not fit the present patterns and schemes of our larger story. Other minor women occasionally appear, but as Elizabeth Cady Stanton comments:

> In the four following books, from Kings to Esther, there is no mention of women. During that long, eventful period the men must have sprung, Minerva-like, from the brains of their fathers, fully armed and equipped for the battle of life. Having no infancy, there was no need of mothers.[6]

Indeed, continuing on from Job to Malachi, we hear little mention of women. We hear briefly of Job's daughters, of the ideal woman of the Proverbs, of first Isaiah's companion called "prophetess," and of Hosea's "wife of harlotry," Gomer. A few other names occasionally rise to the surface, but for the most part, women are largely excluded from the storytelling, politicking, and history of later Israel.

We should, however, take heart for the mention and memory of our foremothers whose history has been recorded, whether in part or full: for Sarah laughing at the angels; for Rebekah masterminding a clever disguise; for Rachel sitting on her father's images; for Tamar sitting by the roadside; for Miriam dancing and singing; for the daughters of Zelophehad requesting property; for Deborah's strength, Hannah's song, Huldah's prophecy; for daughters, wives, sisters, mothers, queens, and prophets: all of the women of Israel.

·II·

WOMAN AND JESUS

SIX

Women of the Gospels

1. Woman who touches Jesus' garment and is healed. **2.** Gentile woman of great faith; daughter healed by Jesus. **3.** Woman who washes Jesus' feet with her hair. **4.** Younger sister from Bethany; quiet, contemplative nature. **5.** Older sister from Bethany; active, busy nature. **6.** Woman healed on the Sabbath; called daughter of Abraham. **7.** Woman of many husbands; talks with Jesus about living water. **8.** Woman brought before Jesus to be stoned. **9.** Close companion of Jesus; first to see him on resurrection morning.

> Rather should the words of the Torah be burned than entrusted to a woman . . . . Whoever teaches his daughter the Torah is like one who teaches her lasciviousness.[1] (Eliezer, 1st c. rabbi)

At the time of Jesus women are far from freedom. Gerhard Kittel, New Testament scholar, claims Judaism involved more reaction than progress. Further, he says, woman is openly despised. Women are called greedy, inquisitive, lazy, vain, and frivolous. Rabbinic quotes concerning women are pointed:

> Happy is he whose children are males, and woe to him whose children are females.

> Ten gab of empty-headedness have come upon the world, nine having been received by women and one by the rest of the world.

> Many women, much witchcraft.[2]

In all areas of living, women remain highly restricted:

Torah. Women were not allowed to study the scriptures. The words of the Torah were to be burned before they would be handed over to a woman. The father who taught his daughter the Torah, was one who taught her extravagance.

Prayer and worship. Because of their low status, women were not required to recite daily prayers, as were the men. The Talmud says: "Let a curse come upon the man whose wife or children say grace for him." Furthermore, included in daily prayers was this thanksgiving:

> Praised be God that he has not created me a gentile; praised be God that he has not created me a woman; praised be God that he has not created me an ignorant man.

Women were also restricted in public prayer; they were not even included in the number necessary for a congregational quorum. In the synagogues women were assigned special places behind a screen, separate from the men; they were not allowed to read aloud or take any leading function.[3]

Private and public lives. In later practice women were secluded by veils and confinement to the home, although they did attend synagogue, the great festivals, and other social occasions. Women could not bear legal witness. Rabbis did not speak to women in public, nor did they greet their own wives, daughters, or mothers. The function of a married woman was to manage the household and bear and raise children. Women were not permitted to divorce their husbands, although the opposite was both true and relatively easy.

Into this world, then, comes Jesus, and with him we see the beginnings of change. Several women are involved with Jesus before his actual ministry begins: Elizabeth, mother of John the Baptist; Anna the prophetess; Mary his mother. For the purposes of this discussion, however, we shall be considering only those women who are with Jesus during his years of teaching, healing, and ministry.

Our stories come from the gospels of Matthew, Mark, Luke, and John. The word gospel, *ευαγγελον* from the Greek, means good tidings, or good news. The gospels in themselves are not historical, factual accounts of the life and events surrounding Jesus. Rather, they give us faith reports, as seen through four different lenses, and prejudiced by four quite different personalities. The source we call Special Luke, for instance, has a particular concern for the poor, the outcast, women, and non-Jews. Mark, considered to be the earliest of the gospels, generally contains fewer details and embellishments, and is closer to the original story source. John contains later stories, often highly symbolic, and bearing essential truths.

Three of the gospels, Matthew, Mark, and Luke, are referred to as the synoptics, (from the Greek, to "see together") because they contain similar or like material. The fourth gospel, John, is an independent and later source. We cannot be certain who the authors of these writings are, but scholarship confirms that the gospels were not written directly from personal reminiscence.[4]

In addition, the synoptic gospels were composed from varying sources, both oral and written, the written being lost. According to Professor Reginald H. Fuller, many levels of tradition may weave themselves into a given account: (1) authentic Jesus tradition—his actual words and work; (2) post-Easter recollection—how the early community interpreted past events; (3) collection of like units of material (parables, for instance); (4) primary written and unwritten collections, such as Mark and Special Luke; (5) later sources, such as Matthew.[5]

Many of the gospel stories on women appear in varying versions. For our discussion, then, we will consider the original material. The gospel accounts themselves present no negative attitudes toward women, an astounding and telling fact. Leonard Swidler, in his paper "Jesus Was a Feminist," comments:

> For whatever Jesus said or did comes to us only through the lens of the first Christians . . . . The fact that the overwhelmingly negative attitude toward women in Palestine did not come through the primitive Christian communal lens by itself underscores the clearly great religious importance Jesus attached to his positive attitude . . . toward women.[6]

What Swidler says is the essential focus of our concentration: the stories may be many-layered, with various levels of interpretation, but the spirit of truth remains. Jesus was unconventional in his attitude towards women; his actions were quite unacceptable to those used to tradition and custom. For most of all, he broke the mold: touching the unclean, healing the crippled, teaching the curious, speaking to, forgiving, and loving the unsung and unknown: women of Judaism. We turn, then, to the change.

The Woman with a Hemorrhage

> For she said, "If I touch even his garments, I shall be made well." And immediately the hemorrhage ceased; and she felt in her body that she was healed of her disease. (Mark 5:28, 29)

All three synoptic gospels report the story of the woman with an issue of blood. Jesus is on his way to see Jairus' daughter, at the request of the distraught Jairus, a ruler of the synagogue. A great crowd follows Jesus and Jairus and the disciples. In the crowd is a woman who has suffered a flow of blood for twelve years; she has seen many physicians, spent all she has, and is "no better but rather grew worse." Hearing the reports about Jesus, she decides to do a daring thing: she comes up behind him in the crowd and touches his clothing. For, she says to herself, this will make me well. Immediately she is healed. Jesus, feeling some power spent, turns to the crowd: "who touched my garments?" The disciples are aghast: "You see the crowd pressing around you, and yet you say, 'Who touched me?'" But Jesus persists and eventually the woman creeps forward, confessing her act. Daughter, says Jesus, your faith has made you well; go in peace, and be healed.

How sweet those words must have sounded in the woman's ears, for Jesus does astounding things: he cleanses her, he speaks with her, he names her, and he gives her peace. The woman is a ritually unclean person, an outcast. She cannot take part in cultic functions, and for years no one would touch anything she herself had touched. Leviticus unequivocally states the result of bodily discharges:

> If a woman has a discharge of blood for many days, not at the time of her impurity, or if she has a discharge beyond the time of her impurity, all the days of her discharge she shall continue in uncleanness . . . . Every bed on which she lies, all the days of her discharge, shall be to her as the bed of her impurity; and everything on which she sits shall be unclean . . . . And whoever touches these things shall be unclean, and shall wash his clothes, and bathe himself in water . . . . (Leviticus 15:25–27)

Quite naturally, then, the woman would fear telling Jesus of her malady, for her actions would have caused him also to be unclean. Jesus seems unconcerned with such possibilities. He speaks with her openly, another taboo, as rabbi figures did not converse with women publicly, and he calls her daughter. After calling her an honorable name he sends her in peace: something the woman has not known in many years. She is cleansed, healed, and given new life.

Reading
Mark 5:25–34
Matthew 9:20–22
Luke 8:43–48
Leviticus 15:25–30

The Syrophoenician Woman

> Now the woman was a Greek, a Syrophoenician by birth. And she begged him to cast the demon out of her daughter.
>
> (Mark 7:26)

The story of the Greek woman and Jesus is a disturbing one at first, as it contains a harshness not usually associated with Jesus. The story opens with Jesus traveling in the region of Tyre and Sidon; he enters a house, hoping his presence will remain unknown, but he is immediately faced with a woman who falls at his feet. She says that her small daughter is possessed by an unclean spirit, and she begs Jesus to heal her. The story makes a point to say that the woman is a Syrophoenician, or non-Jew. Jesus' response is curt: "Let the children first be fed, for it is not right to take the children's bread and throw it to the dogs." The woman answers: "yes, Lord; yet even the dogs under the table eat the children's crumbs." Jesus, pleased with her response, tells her to go her way; the demon has left her daughter. The woman returns home, and the demon is gone.

The story is curious, and it is difficult to discern its original intent. It is clear that Jesus refers to the Jews as children and the Gentiles as dogs. In its primitive form the story may have served as an object lesson for prejudiced Jewish disciples, according to Evelyn and Frank Stagg in *Woman in the World of Jesus.*[7] Regardless of the story's original intent, the woman eventually wins the contest. The Staggs comment:

> . . . noteworthy in this story is the way Jesus appears to be bested in repartee with the Syrophoenician woman. Elsewhere in the Gospels, Jesus uniformly prevails over his opponents . . . . What-

> ever else the story may imply, it has it that a foreign woman comes out victorious and vindicated.[8]

Indeed, in the Matthean version Jesus says: "O woman, great is your faith!" When we recall the Old Testament attitude of suspicion and contempt for foreign women, Jesus' attitude presents a sharp contrast. The woman's daughter is healed, and she is accorded respect and worth from Jesus.

Reading
Mark 7:25–30
Matthew 15:21–28

A Woman of the City

> And behold, a woman of the city, who was a sinner . . . brought an alabaster flask of ointment, and standing before him at his feet, weeping, she began to wet his feet with her tears . . . .
> (Luke 7:37, 38)

In all four gospels there appears a story of a woman who anoints Jesus. The varying details are quite interesting: in Mark and Matthew the place is Bethany, at the home of Simon the leper. In Luke the location is omitted, and Simon becomes a Pharisee. In John the place is Bethany again, this time at the home of Martha, Mary, and Lazarus, and the woman anointing is Mary. In Mark and Matthew the head of Jesus is anointed; in Luke and John the feet are anointed. The point of the story, as reported by Mark, Matthew, and John, is the anointing of Jesus' body before burial. Luke has quite a different emphasis, that of forgiving a sinful woman, and it is to this story we now turn.

Simon the Pharisee asks Jesus to eat with him, and Jesus does. As Jesus and other guests recline at table, a woman enters, bearing an alabaster flask of ointment. She is described as being from the city, and a sinner. She stands behind Jesus and begins to weep, her tears falling on his feet; she wipes his feet with her hair, kisses them and anoints them with oil.

Simon the host is disturbed. If this man were truly a prophet, he says to himself, he would know what kind of woman is touching him. "Simon, I have something to say to you," says Jesus. "What is it, Teacher?" responds Simon. Jesus tells him a story: A certain creditor has two debtors, one owing a good deal of money, the other a lesser amount. They could not pay, and the man forgave them both. Which of the debtors will love the man more? asks Jesus. Simon answers, the one most forgiven.

Jesus then rebukes Simon: Simon gave him no water for his feet, but the woman gave her tears; Simon gave no kiss, but the woman gave in abundance; Simon did not anoint Jesus' head, but the woman has anointed his feet. Jesus turns to the woman: "Your sins are forgiven," he says. The guests are appalled. Who is this who forgives sins? they murmur among themselves. Jesus tells the woman her faith has saved her; she may now go in peace.

Once again Jesus astounds those about him. He strongly defends a woman who is a "sinner"; we are not told of her sins, but it is fair speculation that she is a prostitute. Her touching Jesus would render him unclean, but as with the woman of the hemorrhage, his unconcern is apparent. He defends the woman, he speaks with her openly, and he commits a final trespass: he forgives her. This itself is shocking enough to Simon and his guests, for God alone forgives sins. Luke's emphasis, then, is not on anointing or on burial, but on the forgiveness of a reputed sinner, a woman. Jesus lifts her to new dignity, pronounces her sins forgiven, sends her on her way in peace.

Reading
Luke 7:36–50
Mark 14:3–9
Matthew 26:6–13
John 12:1–8

Mary and Martha

> Now as they went on their way, he entered a village; and a woman named Martha received him into her house. And she had a sister named Mary, who sat at the Lord's feet and listened to his teaching. (Luke 10:38, 39)

Luke is the only gospel telling the small story of Mary at Jesus' feet. Jesus is journeying with his friends, and they enter a village. Martha opens her house to the travelers and begins to prepare a meal. Mary, her sister, sits at Jesus' feet while he teaches. Unsettled with so much serving, Martha approaches Jesus: "Lord, do you not care that my sister has left me to serve alone? Tell her then to help me." "Martha,

Martha," Jesus replies, "you are anxious and troubled about many things." He tells her that one thing is needful: Mary has chosen the good portion which is rightfully hers.

The story in itself is not one we would notice at first glance: an older sister is disgruntled with her younger sister, and Jesus settles the trouble. Yet there is more. The hospitality code was of no small importance to the Jewish people; the women of the household were expected to entertain their guests with refreshment and tend to their needs. Mary blatantly chooses another role. Even more surprising, Jesus accepts it. For Mary is doing the unprecedented: she sits at the feet of a teacher, a rabbi, in the company of men, and receives his teaching and religious instruction. As women were not permitted to touch the Torah or be instructed in its words, Mary's actions were a distinct break with Jewish custom. Jesus must have encouraged her; indeed, there may have been several women present in the room.

Luke records that many women were regular followers of Jesus, people who ministered to his needs and listened to his teaching and preaching:

> Soon afterward he went on through cities and villages, preaching and bringing the good news . . . . And the twelve were with him, and also some women . . . Mary, called Magdalene . . . and Joanna . . . and Susanna, and many others, who provided for them out of their means. (Luke 8:1–3)

This passage becomes highly important when we realize that women simply did not roam about the countryside, according to custom. They were to remain at home, caring for their families. This behavior, then, must have been as surprising to onlookers as Mary's behavior was to Martha. Yet we nowhere have an indication that Jesus discourages the presence of women in his company. On the contrary, he teaches them, travels with them, accepts their comfort and companionship.

Reading

Luke 10:38–42
(John 11:1–44)
(John 12:1–8) other stories of Mary and Martha

The Crooked Woman

> And there was a woman who had a spirit of infirmity for eighteen years; she was bent over and could not fully straighten herself. (Luke 13:11)

The crooked woman, or the woman bent double, is a story rarely heard. It is not among the readings of major ecumenical lectionaries, and therefore would not be included in yearly Sunday lessons. Commentaries past and present generally ignore this small story, except for an occasional listing. The crooked woman is virtually unknown. Yet hers is an especially poignant tale, for the light and the power of Jesus and woman shines through in the telling.

The story opens with Jesus teaching in one of the synagogues; it is the sabbath. Jesus sees the crippled woman who cannot straighten herself, and he calls. "Woman," he says, "you are freed from your infirmity." He then lays his hands upon her; immediately she is made straight, and she praises God.

But the ruler of the synagogue is indignant. There are six working days, he says; come then to be healed, not on the sabbath. Jesus meets his anger:

> You hypocrites! Does not each of you on the sabbath untie his ox or his ass from the manger, and lead it away to water it? And ought not this woman, a daughter of Abraham whom Satan bound for eighteen years, be loosed from this bond on the sabbath day? (Luke 13:15, 16)

After this saying Jesus' adversaries are quieted, and all the people rejoice over the glorious work done.

The crooked woman's story is brief but telling. First, Jesus calls her. As far as we know, she does nothing to attract his attention. Jesus is moved with pity by this disfigured woman, and it is he who initiates a meeting. This is all the more remarkable when we recall the separateness of the synagogue for women and men. Either Jesus went to the women's court, or he called the woman into the men's section.

Secondly, Jesus touches her. He gives the woman startling news: you are freed. Then he reaches out and pours compassion and healing into the crippled body. Having had a "spirit of infirmity" for a lengthy time, the woman is regarded by others as filled with demons. Jesus also attributes her disorder to the work of Satan. She therefore is unclean, untouchable, yet again Jesus reaches out to touch as he does with others: Jairus' daughter (Mark 5:41), the deaf man (Mark 7:33), the blind man (Mark 8:22), the leper (Mark 1:41), the two blind men (Matthew 20:34), the epileptic child (Mark 9:22). In many instances, when Jesus touches people the story also mentions his compassion. From the Greek, compassion literally means "to have the bowels ache." Jesus ached for the brokenness in people, the crooked woman included, and he reached out and made her whole.

Third, Jesus names the woman. As with the woman who touched his robe, Jesus calls this woman *daughter*, yet now we see the completion of the title: daughter of Abraham. This address is unusual. G. Kittel notes:

> The honorable title of "daughter of Abraham" is rare in Rabbinic literature as compared with the corresponding "son of Abraham."[9]

We often hear of "sons of Abraham," the "seed of Abraham," or "children of Abraham,"[10] but Luke alone records this special naming; the title appears nowhere else in the New Testament. Jesus has included the infirm woman in the family of Israel: she is daughter, part of the community, a recognized human being.

Lastly, and most obvious, Jesus heals the woman on the sabbath. To understand the enormity of this we need to recall the strict codes of the sabbath; there was to be no work done at all on this day of rest. Numbers relates the story of a man who gathered sticks on the sabbath:

> While the people of Israel were in the wilderness, they found a man gathering sticks on the sabbath day. And those who found him gathering sticks brought him to Moses and Aaron and to all the congregation . . . . And the Lord said to Moses, "The man shall be put to death; all the congregation shall stone him with stones outside the camp." (Numbers 15:32–34)

The man was stoned, by the entire congregation. Thus the intensity of the synagogue ruler's response, for Jesus is doing work on the sabbath—healing—and the people are participating. It is flagrant wrongdoing, and must be stopped. Yet Jesus counters: do you not untie and water your animals on the sabbath? and should not this woman be loosed?

Another woman, then, is lifted up for all to see. Not only is she healed on the sabbath, but she is called and touched and named as well. The crooked woman, bound so long, is loosed at last. She is healed, she is whole, and she is free.

Reading
Luke 13:10–17

The Well Woman

> There came a woman of Samaria to draw water. Jesus said to her, "Give me a drink" . . . . The Samaritan woman said to him, "How is it that you, a Jew, ask a drink of me, a woman of Samaria?" (John 4:7, 9)

With the story of the woman at the well we shift to the gospel of John. Although the historical details in this gospel are often called into question, we can say with certainty that this is the longest recorded conversation Jesus has with anyone, and it carries essential truths.

Jesus and his friends are traveling from southern Judea to northern Galilee. On the way, they pass through the middle land of Samaria. The sun is high, and they find a very old well, in a field. Jesus, quite weary, sits down next to this well of Jacob, and the disciples go into the city of Sychar to buy food. A woman appears with her jug, intending to draw water. Jesus asks her for a drink. She is confused by his request, for Jews do not associate with Samaritans, as she says. They begin a conversation about the water, the woman interpreting the water literally, and Jesus speaking of living water. Jesus says whoever drinks the water he gives will never thirst; the water will become "a spring of water welling up . . . ." The woman responds:

> Sir, give me this water, that I may not thirst, nor come here to draw. (John 4:15)

Jesus tells her to call her husband. The woman says she has none. Yes, Jesus says, for you have had five and now live unmarried with another. "Sir," says the woman, "I perceive you are a prophet." The conversation continues with a discussion of places of worship: Mount Gerizim for the Samaritans and Jerusalem for the Jews. Jesus tells the woman the place of worship will have no importance in the coming kingdom, and he speaks of himself as the Messiah to come.

The disciples return; they are surprised that Jesus is talking with a woman, but they do not ask why. The woman leaves her water jar, goes to the city, and tells the people of the man by the well. Can this be the Christ? she says; he has told me all that I have ever done. The people, then, come to Jesus.

With the well woman Jesus once again shatters Jewish custom. The woman is astounded that he speaks with her, both because she is a woman and also a Samaritan. Custom did not allow a rabbi to speak publicly with a woman. The disciples are then confused when they return with food and find Jesus conversing with the well woman. The story says "they marveled."

Jews also held Samaritans in contempt. They simply did not associate one with another. In traveling from Judea to Galilee most Jews would circumvent the Samaritan territory rather than pass through, yet Jesus chose the direct route. Samaritans, in Jewish eyes, were religious apostates, dating back to the time of the Assyrian captivity:

> And the king of Assyria brought people from Babylon, Cuthah, Avva, Hamath, and Sepharvaim, and placed them in the cities of Samaria instead of the people of Israel; and they took possession of Samaria, and dwelt in its cities. And at the beginning of their dwelling there, they did not fear the Lord.
>
> (II Kings 17:24, 25a)

Jesus' action, drinking from the same jar as a Samarian, is highly unorthodox. The woman, at first surprised, soon warms to the conversation, only to change it when she becomes personally too uncomfortable. For Jesus sees her clearly, as if holding a mirror to her face; he knows of her husbands and of her transgressions. He judges her, yet he does not condemn her. They talk of their respective places of worship, and Jesus explains the meaning of true worship. The woman, enlivened by the conversation, leaves the water jar in her haste to reach the city.

Jesus again has small concern for honored custom. Rather than sit by the well in silence, he chooses to speak with a strange woman, one not of his community and tradition. She seems to delight in him and he openly cares to teach her. There is no hesitation: the woman is important to Jesus, a person of worth, one he chooses to use as an emissary to other Samaritans. The woman herself, then, becomes a teacher. She is heard and respected: the living water fills her.

Reading
John 4:1–42

The Adulterous Woman

> The scribes and the Pharisees brought a woman who had been caught in adultery, and placing her in the midst they said to him, "Teacher, this woman has been caught in the act of adultery. Now in the law Moses commanded us to stone such. What do you say about her?" (John 8:3–5)

The account in John 7:53 – 8:11 of the woman caught in adultery has long been considered not originally a part of John's gospel. The story, however, appears to be an authentic incident in Jesus' ministry, and a well-loved and much-remembered tale.

The story opens in a flurry of action: Jesus is teaching a crowd in the temple; the religious leaders interrupt him, dragging in a woman just caught in adultery. They challenge Jesus: Moses says to stone her, they say; what do you say? Jesus doesn't say anything. Instead, he bends in the dust and begins to write with his finger on the ground. The scribes and Pharisees continue to ask the question. Jesus stands and looks at them:

> Let him who is without sin among you be the first to throw a stone at her. (John 8:7)

Then he bends again and writes in the dust. The leaders begin to slip away, one by one, beginning with the eldest. The woman and Jesus are left alone. "Woman, where are they?" asks Jesus. "Has no one condemned you?" "No one Lord," she says. "Nor do I condemn you," says Jesus; "Go, and do not sin again."

The scribes and Pharisees do all they can to trap Jesus. The woman is almost incidental, for they are hoping to snag Jesus on a legality.

And certainly the Jewish law was quite pointed concerning sexual offenses:

> If a man commits adultery with the wife of his neighbor, both the adulterer and the adulteress shall be put to death.
>
> (Leviticus 20:10)

> If there is a betrothed virgin, and a man meets her in the city and lies with her, then you shall bring them both out to the gate of that city, and you shall stone them to death with stones, the young woman because she did not cry for help . . . and the man because he violated his neighbor's wife . . .
>
> (Deuteronomy 22:23, 24)

It is not clear in this instance whether the woman is married or unmarried, or who exactly is at fault; regardless, she is to be fully punished for her offense. The most telling fact is the omission of her consort: the man is nowhere mentioned and nowhere accused. According to law, he, too, should be stoned. Yet the woman is clearly the center of accusation.

The book of Numbers also gives detailed instructions for a woman suspected of adultery. In this instance, the woman is brought to the priest and forced to go through a ritual trial: the priest gives her "water of bitterness" to drink, a potion designed to disease the body if there is guilt.

> . . . "the Lord make you an execration and an oath among your people, when the Lord makes your thigh fall away and your body swell; may this water that brings the curse pass into your bowels and make your body swell and your thigh fall away." And the woman shall say, "Amen, Amen." (Numbers 5:21, 22)

There is no mention here of men committing adultery, nor any detailed punishment such as this, for the man. And there is no way for the woman to avoid drinking the bitter water, guilty or not.

These considerations and traditions, then, lie behind the question to Jesus: what do you say? Jesus, with characteristic aplomb, writes in the dust instead of answering. According to several later manuscripts, Jesus writes on the ground the sins of each of them. Seeing these, the accusers are reduced to silence. Jesus then speaks gently with the woman, and she goes her way.

The boldness of Jesus' action remains evident, however quietly handled. He does not argue or defend; he simply dismisses the stoning. Further, he forgives the woman in an unprecedented manner. She is not without sin, yet Jesus chooses not to condemn her, for she has been shamed enough. The woman's life is saved; she is of value, a restored member of the community.

Reading
John 7:53 – 8:11
Deuteronomy 22:22 ff
Numbers 5:16 ff

Mary Magdalene

> Jesus said to her, "Woman, why are you weeping? Whom do you seek?" Supposing him to be the gardener, she said to him, "Sir, if you have carried him away, tell me where you have laid him, and I will take him away." Jesus said to her, "Mary."
> (John 20:15, 16a)

Jesus touched, healed, defended, and forgave many women, but Mary was a close companion. Many have speculated on the association of Mary Magdalene and Jesus, and canonical scripture reveals a probable intimate friendship. One uncanonical quote, from the gospel of Philip, has Mary as a source of discontent and jealousy for the other disciples:

> . . . the companion of the [Savior is] Mary Magdalene. [But Christ loved] her more than [all] the disciples, and used to kiss her [often] on her [mouth]. The rest of [the disciples were offended] . . . They said to him, "Why do you love her more than all of us?" The Savior answered and said to them, "Why do I not love you as (I love) her?"[11] (Gospel of Philip 63:32–64:5)

What truth there is in this is difficult to say. Early on, the Gospel of Philip was not accepted as legitimate, by the orthodox, because of its gnostic tendencies. But it is interesting that over the centuries Mary has borne much speculation and judgment, from all sides. She is almost universally accepted as a prostitute, whereas scripture gives no indication of this. The only mention of her previous life appears in Luke 8:2: "Mary, called Magdalene, from whom seven demons had gone out . . ." The demons are not explained. A preceding passage, Luke 7:36–50, speaks of the woman of the city, a sinner, and it is with this woman that Mary Magdalene has been so closely identified. There is no evidence to support this.

What we do know is that Mary is mentioned more than any other woman in the New Testament. She apparently comes from Magdala, on the Sea of Galilee. In Mark we hear of her at the crucifixion; she is described as one of the women who follows Jesus and ministers to him. She also sees where Jesus is laid, and is one of the women to bring spices to the tomb, after the sabbath. Mark records that when Jesus rises, he appears first to Mary Magdalene. She then goes to tell the others, but they will not believe her.

Luke mentions Mary traveling with Jesus and other companions, and notes her previous demons. In Luke, also, Mary is among the women at the tomb; she and others tell the disciples of the empty tomb, but they count it an "idle tale." Matthew has Mary at the crucifixion, with other women, and also has her sitting opposite the tomb that evening. She then goes to the tomb at dawn on the first day with "the other Mary." An angel appears to them and sends them back to the disciples; on the way Jesus meets them.

The synoptic gospels, then, all make mention of women following and ministering to Jesus, and being present both at his death and after his rising. The women's names vary from source to source, but Mary Magdalene's presence is consistent. She stands out as close companion, faithful friend.

The gospel of John gives a full story of Mary and Jesus after the resurrection. Mary has been at the cross with Jesus' mother, his mother's sister, and others. Jesus is now dead, his body taken down from the cross, as it could not remain on the sabbath. It is the day of Preparation for the Passover. Joseph of Arimathea, a disciple of Jesus and elsewhere described as "a rich man," and "a respected member of the council," goes to Pilate and asks for Jesus' body. Pilate gives him leave. Nicodemus also comes, bringing myrrh and aloes for the burial. The men wrap the body in linen cloths and spices, and place it in a new tomb, in a garden. It is now evening, the beginning of the sabbath.

On the first day of the week, after sabbath, Mary Magdalene comes to the tomb early, while it is yet dark. Seeing the stone gone she runs to Peter and another disciple in panic: "They have taken the Lord out of the tomb, and we do not know where they have laid him." The disciples run to the tomb, peer in, and see the linen cloths lying about. Then they go back home.

But Mary stands outside the tomb, weeping. As she looks into the tomb she sees two angels who ask her why she weeps. "Because they have taken away my Lord," she says, "and I do not know where they have laid him." She then turns to see Jesus, only she does not know it is Jesus. He, too, asks her why she weeps. Thinking him the gardener, Mary asks if he has carried away the body. Jesus answers with her name: Mary. She turns in astonishment and says, "Rabboni!", Teacher. Then she goes to tell the disciples: I have seen the Lord, she says, and tells them all of Jesus.

Although it is difficult to measure the accuracy of this particular account in John's gospel, essential truth remains: Mary is unsurpassed in her devotion to Jesus. Other disciples have come and gone back home, but Mary stays close by, weeping. Her loss is great, for she has been with Jesus from the beginning. She has seen him heal, heard him teach, felt power in his presence. She herself has been healed by him. Yet Jesus comes to her once more, saying her name. And in the name sounds comfort and healing and love.

The gospel of John, then, records unparalleled intimacy between teacher and follower, lord and disciple, friend and friend. The other gospels, too, give evidence of a close association between Mary and Jesus. This kind of friendship would be unheard-of in conventional Judaism, and would suggest a clear break with custom. It is not surprising, then, that some would be offended by Jesus' closeness with Mary, however this was evidenced. Jesus regards Mary as friend, and further entrusts her to carry news to the others; and in a time when a woman's word was suspect, this is extraordinary. Mary Magdalene, then, is companion and comforter and trusted friend, and Jesus raises her as equal among the disciples.

Reading

Mark 15:40, 47
16:1, 9
Luke 8:2
24:10
Matthew 27:56, 61
28:1
John 19:25
20:1–18

Other Women

We do not wish to leave the gospels without mentioning other women. The gospel of Mark speaks of Peter's mother-in-law, a woman with fever, healed by Jesus; Jairus' daughter, a small child raised by Jesus; a poor widow praised by Jesus. The gospel of Luke contains the story of the widow of Nain, whose only son is raised by Jesus; the parable of a woman and a lost coin, the woman portraying God; the parable of a widow before an unjust judge.

Never in the gospels does Jesus speak disparagingly of a woman, nor is there the slightest hint that woman is somehow less than man. Jesus makes no mention of the early creation story. Reference to woman as Eve or evil does not hold place in his consideration. Rather, Jesus' actions verify Genesis 1:27: woman and man equal in creation, both in the image of God. Jesus shows us rather than tells us: he touches the outcast, heals the crippled, forgives the sinful, teaches, speaks with, and befriends the women of the gospels: they in turn, follow him and minister to him, and wait on him at death.

Reading

Mark 1:30, 31	Peter's mother-in-law
5:21–24; 35–43	Jairus' daughter
12:41–44	poor widow
Luke 7:11–17	widow of Nain
15:8–10	woman and lost coin
18:1–8	widow and unjust judge

The Twelve

Gerhard Kittel notes that Jesus ". . . lifts from woman the curse of her sex and sets her at the side of man as equally a child of God."[12] This, then, brings us to a further consideration: if this is true, and if the gospel accounts are indeed transparent with the truth of women and Jesus, why, then, do we not hear mention of women disciples?

The fact is, we do. We hear of Mary and Martha and Mary Magdalene and Susanna and Joanna and others. They are often referred to with the twelve, but not included in the numbering. Women were often not included in the numbering. Dinah, for instance, was present in the crossing of the river Jabbok, but not included in the counting of the children, all boys. During the time of Moses, women were not counted in the census taken in the wilderness, excepting the daughters of Zelophehad. In Jesus' time, women were not included in the number of four thousand fed: "Those who ate were four thousand men, besides women and children." (Matthew 15:38) And in later times women were not included in the numbering of a congregational quorum. Present, but not counted. It should not be surprising, then, that women disciples of Jesus were continually present, but not numbered. Certainly Mary, Martha, Mary, Susanna, and Joanna were among the inner circle.

Further, it is necessary to regard the number of twelve itself as having a meaning particular to the people of Israel. The New Testament holds four counts of male disciples, all with variations, and all totalling twelve (cf. Mark 3:13–19; Luke 6:12–16; Matthew 10:1–4; Acts 1:13). The number twelve was a powerful symbol for Israel, for the sons of Jacob (and Rachel and Leah and Zilpah and Bilhah) became the twelve tribes of Israel. Jacob, called "Israel," and his sons' ancestors led the people out of Egypt, back home to the promised land. The parallel becomes clear: early writers saw Jesus as the new Moses, and the twelve were those who would once again release the people of Israel. From bondage to deliverance, led by the sons.

This is one feasible explanation. Another less likely explanation is to consider the twelve as literal, and credit lack of women disciples to cultural fact. For, as we have seen, women did not mingle freely with men. Certainly they did not travel with them, gather with them, worship with them, or learn with them. Yet the experience with Jesus, as seen through the early writers' eyes, does not verify this; Jesus broke rigid custom with startling regularity. It is not unsafe to assume, then, that women were also numbered among the disciples. We would certainly hope this to be true, and the activity of women in the early church would further indicate full inclusion.

·III·

WOMAN AND THE EARLY CHURCH

SEVEN

Women of Acts and Letters of Paul

1. Woman of good works and charity; sews for widows at Joppa; brought to life by Peter. **2.** Woman whose home in Jersualem is a center of prayer; mother of John called Mark. **3.** Merchant of Philippi: seller of purple goods; she and household baptized by Paul; has house church which she heads. **4.** Tentmaker and teacher of Corinth and Ephesus; travels with Paul and husband Aquila; heads a house church. **5.** Four married daughters who prophesy. **6.** Honored deacon of the church at Cenchreae; called a helper of many. **7.** Two women in the church at Philippi who labored side by side with Paul.

Then they returned to Jerusalem from the mount called Olivet . . . and when they had entered, they went up to the upper room, where they were staying, Peter and John and James and Andrew, Philip and Thomas, Bartholomew and Matthew, James . . . and Simon . . . and Judas . . . All these with one accord devoted themselves to prayer, together with the women and Mary the mother of Jesus, and with his brothers. (Acts 1:12–14)

There is no doubt, in the early community, as to the full membership of women.[1] Women and men now meet together, pray together, learn together, and serve a common people. The book of Acts, called the Acts of the Apostles, and several early letters of Paul make mention of a number of women. Jesus' positive, life-giving response to women begins to take root, and we see a blossoming in the community of early times. There appears, however, to be a greater freedom given to women in the gospels than in the letters, or epistles. Acts, long thought to be an extended work of Luke, preserves a similar gospel attitude toward women.

Although the letters of Paul are thought to have been written earlier than the gospels or Acts, they reflect rules and regulations for women which nowhere appear in the gospels and Acts. A possible explanation for this is that the gospel writers faithfully preserved Jesus' ministry and attitude toward women, even though they wrote some time after the letters.[2] The letters, both by St. Paul and by later writers attributed to St. Paul, contain a variety of positive and negative attitudes toward women. These opinions seem to often depend on the writer's own bias concerning women, and are not necessarily akin to Jesus'unorthodox position. The times were confusing, and in some respects disorderly, and freedom and order seemed to be bound together with women of the early community. Let us, then, look to the positive side first, as we consider women in the story of Acts, and women associated with St. Paul.

I

The Acts of the Apostles begins with an introductory note to Theophilus, an unknown person, who is also mentioned in the opening of the gospel of Luke:

> In the first book, O Theophilus, I have delt with all that Jesus began to do and teach, until the day when he was taken up after he had given commandment through the Holy Spirit to the apostles whom he had chosen. (Acts 1:1, 2)

The book of Acts continues the story of Jesus, as first told in Luke's gospel. We hear of the risen Christ, the day of Pentecost, the community of believers in Jerusalem, the conversion of Paul, and his subsequent missionary journeys. The book ends with Paul's arrival in Rome, and his teaching and preaching there. In between these events we learn a good deal about the women and men of early times: where they met, how they worshipped, whom they followed, what they believed. Several women are mentioned in the story of Acts, although

Peter and Paul are the dominant characters. Authors Evelyn and Frank Stagg note that "it is hard to escape the conclusion that Jesus' followers gave less room to women than did Jesus."[3] Although women do receive less attention in Acts than in Luke, they are nevertheless participating members of the community, and valued people. They are involved in community prayer, in teaching and prophecy, in early liturgical functioning, and "co-workers in the Lord." We now turn to the women of the early church.

Tabitha

> Now there was at Joppa a disciple named Tabitha, which means Dorcas. She was full of good works and acts of charity. In those days she died . . . (Acts 9:36, 37a)

Tabitha, a follower of Jesus, suddenly falls ill and dies. The people in her community of Joppa wash her and lay her in an upper room. Some disciples hear that Peter is nearby, and they send an urgent message: Please come to us without delay. Peter then comes and they take him to the upper room. All the widows stand close to him, weeping; they hold up the many tunics and other clothing Tabitha made while she was with them. Peter sends them all away and is alone with the woman's body. He begins to pray: Tabitha, rise, he says. Tabitha opens her eyes, sits up, and Peter lifts her up. He then calls the "saints and widows" and shows them their friend, alive. The tale of the deed spreads through Joppa, and many believe.

The small story of Tabitha, meaning gazelle, is indeed touching. Tabitha, evidently not a widow herself, is called "disciple," this being the only New Testament occurrence of the feminine form of the word disciple.[4] Tabitha's particular ministry seems to be in aiding a group of widows: she is a seamstress for them, and most likely aids them also with her comfort and companionship. Whatever her role, she is considered "full of good works and acts of charity." She is evidently a highly respected person in her community, for when she dies, her friends go straight to Peter, who is by then the undisputed leader of the Jewish-Christian people. That Peter comes is high tribute, and his act of raising her is even a greater deed. Tabitha is the only New Testament person to be raised from the dead by a disciple of Jesus.

The act of Peter raises an interesting question, and is actually an aside to the story of Tabitha. Why did Peter raise Tabitha in the first place? Why are her friends so concerned by her death? The book of I Thessalonians, one of Paul's earliest works, gives us a clue. The people of Thessalonica were quite concerned with death: is a Christian deprived of the blessings of the kingdom if she or he dies before the second coming of Christ? The very early Christian belief was that Jesus the Christ would return in their own life time, and the people awaited his return with great anticipation. So, when Tabitha suddenly dies, it is something of a crisis for the believers in her town. They want to restore her so she will be alive for the coming of the Lord. This early story, then, gives us insight not only into the expanded role of a woman freely ministering, but also into the minds and concerns of people of the early times. Tabitha remains a noted disciple, a charity-filled woman, one who spent her days in the service of others.

Reading
Acts 9:36–43

Mary

> . . . Peter went to the house of Mary, the mother of John whose other name was Mark, where many were gathered together and were praying. (Acts 12:12)

As we move on through the book of Acts, we hear that Herod the king—meaning Herod Agrippa I, made king A.D. 41—begins to lay "violent hands" upon some who belong to the church. James the brother of John is killed with the sword, and Peter is arrested. He is seized, put in prison, and guarded by four squads of soldiers. While Peter is in prison the story says that "earnest prayer for him was made to God by the church."

The very night Peter is to be brought out to the people for judgment a miraculous thing occurs: an angel of the Lord appears, a light shines in Peter's cell, and his chains fall off. The angel disappears, and Peter immediately goes to the house of Mary, where many are gathered, praying. A maid named Rhoda answers his knock at the door, and recognizing his voice, she runs to tell the others. They say she is mad, it cannot be Peter; it must be his angel. But Peter himself enters, and the gathered friends are amazed. He tells them of his wondrous release, and then goes on to another place.

We know next to nothing about the woman Mary in this story, other than that she was the mother of Mark, who is traditionally credited with the writing of the earliest gospel. Yet she here plays another important role, for evidently her home has become a center for meeting, one of the "house churches" of early times. The early Christians, for fear of persecution, often met in private homes for common worship and gathering. It is telling that Peter, after fleeing prison, goes at once to Mary's home. We can assume that hers is a house where the believers met regularly, at the risk of their lives. Various other women's houses were often the first Christian "churches."[5] Several passages suggest this:

> For it has been reported to me by Chloe's people that there is quarreling among you. (I Corinthians 1:11)

> From prison they went to Lydia's house where they saw all the friends and gave them some encouragement. (Acts 16:40)

> Please give my greetings to the friends at Laodicea and to Nympha and the church which meets at her house.
> (Colossians 4:15)

> My greetings to Prisca and Aquila . . . . my greetings also to the church that meets in their house. (Romans 16:3,5)

Men are not mentioned as being heads of house churches, save a listing in Philemon (1, 2), where Philemon is named, along with a woman, Apphia. The other mention is Aquila, in connection with Priscilla. Women, then, are becoming leaders in the early community; their homes are regular meeting places, and we can assume they actively participated in the worship.

And lest we forget the obvious, the brief passage on the house of Mary makes it clear that women and men are now praying as a community. No longer do we have a women's court, and the court of Israel, for "many were gathered together and were praying." This is an astounding breach of custom. Jesus' influence here is widely felt, as the people continue his practice. The house of Mary and the other women's houses are revolutionary: they house dissidents, they break custom, they initiate new worship, they continue the teachings of Jesus.

Reading
Acts 12:12
1:14

Lydia

> We remained in this city [Philippi] some days; and on the sabbath day we went outside the gate to the riverside, where we supposed there was a place of prayer; and we sat down and spoke to the women who had come together. One who heard us was a woman named Lydia, from the city of Thyatira, a seller of purple goods, who was a worshipper of God.
>
> (Acts 16:12b–14a)

Paul, on one of his missionary journeys, enters Europe for the first time. He and his friend Silas come to Philippi, the leading city of Macedonia, and a Roman colony. There they meet and speak with a group of women who have come together for worship. One woman is particularly mentioned, Lydia, a seller of purple goods. As she listens to Paul, "the Lord opens her heart" and she believes Paul's words. Paul later baptizes Lydia and her entire household, and she invites him to stay at her house.

Paul and Silas then fall into a series of trials: they agitate some Roman citizens who incite a crowd against them. The crowd tears their clothing, beats them, and throws them into prison; the jailer puts them in an inner prison and fastens their feet in stocks. Around midnight Paul and Silas begin to pray and sing hymns, while the other prisoners listen. Suddenly there is a great earthquake; the prisoners' fetters come unfastened, and the doors open. The jailer is subsequently converted, and he and his household are baptized. Paul and Silas return to prison, claiming that they are Roman citizens and should not be mistreated, and the authorities ask them to leave the city. Before they do so, they make a final visit to Lydia and the believers of her household. They then depart, after some exhortation to the new community.

We know little of Lydia, but what we do know gives rise to interesting speculation. Her story does not mention a husband, nor is she called *widow*. She is evidently a merchant, and a rather wealthy one at that, to be in charge of a considerable household. She is often called the first European convert, and her house becomes a meeting place for the other new believers in Philippi. This gathering evidently continued to flourish, for the New Testament contains a letter to the Philippians, written by Paul. Paul addresses his letter to the "saints in Christ Jesus" at Philippi, along with the "bishops and deacons."

The letter to the Philippians is usually dated around A.D. 61–63. The emergence of the threefold ministry, or the offices of deacon, presbyter, and bishop, did not actually begin until approximately A.D. 110. St. Paul's mention of bishop and deacon is one of the few places in the New Testament where they are at all mentioned. These particular ministries were not yet precisely formed, and their functions and titles were still loosely defined and often interchangeable. We do know there were women deacons in early times, and in this story there is quite possibly a hint of a woman acting as presbyter, or priest.

In the early church, breaking bread together was common practice. Acts describes the early believers' custom:

> And they devoted themselves to the apostles' teaching and fellowship, to the breaking of bread and the prayers. (Acts 2:42)

> And day by day, attending the temple together and breaking bread in their homes, they partook of food with glad and generous hearts. (Acts 2:46)

This act of worship, influenced by Jesus' own last meal, and by the Jewish sabbath meal or *chaburah*,[6] later evolved into the Eucharist, or service of thanksgiving. St. Paul was most certainly aware of this practice, for he speaks of the "cup of blessing which we bless" and "the bread which we break" in I Corinthians 10:16, and he further gives directions concerning the Lord's supper in I Corinthians 11:23–26. Undoubtedly he took these practices with him on his journeys, taught them to new believers, and exhorted them to continue with this cherished custom.

So we return to Lydia, the head of the household. In early days, the head of the household was the usual person to preside over the breaking of bread, in the absence of a noted apostle or visiting person of importance. The household head in Jewish practice was the father, the one who, at the sabbath meal, took a piece of bread, spoke over it a short prayer of blessing, broke it, and distributed the pieces to the guests at table.[7] While the New Testament does not clearly state who among the early Christians actually presides over these "meals," it is safe to assume each community had its household leaders. Many of these, as we have seen, were women, and several were unmarried, as their husbands are not named. It is possible, then, that these women functioned in a role which later was to be called presbyter, or priest. As household heads they assumed a leadership role: they broke the bread, and blessed the cup, and passed it to their guests.

We have further evidence of this in recent discoveries by archaeologist and theologian Dorothy Irvin. Dr. Irvin, a photographer for the Biblical Archaeological Institute at Tubingen for several years, has collected frescoes, mosaics, and inscriptions which provide proof that women functioned as priests and bishops in the early church. Says Irvin:

> Although it is not perfectly clear what constituted ordination at different times and places in the early centuries of the church, archaeological evidence shows women as receiving ordination and exercising ministry on a par with men.[8]

Dr. Irvin goes on to describe her findings:

- Inscriptions from the Roman period, from tombstones or for legal-financial purposes, which name women who bore the titles *archisynagogos,* (ruler of the synagogue), "mother of the synagogue," and *presbitera* (the feminine of presbyter). These titles were used by Jewish, Jewish-Christian, and Christian communities. We have inscriptions of the same type giving men these titles, in the masculine form. We also have burial inscriptions of the wives of men who have such titles. These have a different form from that in which the woman herself bears the title.

- A fresco, dating to the end of the first century, in a Roman catacomb, which depicts a group of seven women celebrating a Eucharist. Several similar scenes from a later date depict groups of seven men.

- A fourth-century catacomb fresco, also in Rome, showing a woman being ordained by a bishop. I do not know of any scenes of the ordination of a man, although all agree that men were ordained at this period!

- Many frescoes of women (as well as men) dressed in liturgical vestments and standing in attitudes of liturgical leadership.

- A mosaic, dating between the fifth and ninth centuries, showing a female head, with superscription, also in mosaic, *Episcopa Theodo(ra),* "bishop (feminine) Theodora." She wears a coif, indicating that she is not married.

- Tombstone inscriptions of women bishops, for example *(hono)rabilis femina episcopa,* "honorable woman bishop."

Irvin continues:

> The orthodoxy of these sources, so far as I am aware, has never been questioned. That is, they have never been identified as Gnostic or Montanist records, i.e., from groups of heretics or schismatics.[9]

Irvin further describes how the fresco of women celebrating a Eucharist has been altered in a later mosaic copy. Most of the women have been changed to men, one with a beard and others with male clothing. Citing another example, Irvin describes how the postcards of the mosaic of Bishop Theodora have darkened the letters of her name and title, rendering them illegible.

Irvin's findings are remarkable. Hope lives in the promise of the evidence, however muddled and unclear it has become over the centuries. Women most certainly functioned as leaders in the early community; doing charitable acts, opening their homes for meetings, and functioning liturgically as well. Lydia is one example, and, when Paul later writes to the growing community at Philippi, the "bishops and deacons" could likely have included the women Paul met by the river: Lydia and her friends, the first Christian believers in Europe.

Reading
Acts 16:11–15, 40
Philippians 1:1

Priscilla

> After this Paul left Athens and went to Corinth. And he found a Jew named Aquila, a native of Pontus, lately come from Italy with his wife Priscilla . . . . (Acts 18:1,2)

Priscilla, or Prisca as she is called, is mentioned some six times in the New Testament. She is always listed with her husband, Aquila, and in four out of the six times, her name appears first. Priscilla and Aquila become traveling companions of Paul, and "co-workers" in his ministry. We hear of them in Acts as Paul leaves Athens and goes to Corinth. Here he finds Priscilla and Aquila, Jews lately come from Rome. As they all share the same trade, tentmaking, they soon live and work together. Paul, arguing in the synagogue every sabbath, persuades many Jews and Greeks.

After this Paul leaves the growing community at Corinth, sails for Syria, and Priscilla and Aquila go with him. They eventually come to Ephesus; here Paul leaves his new friends and sails for other parts. In the meantime, a Jew named Apollos comes to Ephesus; he is an eloquent man, well versed in the scriptures. Further, he has been "instructed in the way of the Lord" and is "fervent in spirit," yet he is unfamiliar with certain rites such as baptism in Jesus' name. When Priscilla and Aquila hear him speaking boldly in the synagogue, they take him aside and teach him the way of God more accurately.

Priscilla and Aquila also appear in two of Paul's letters, Romans and I Corinthians, and in another letter, II Timothy, written by a later author:

> Greet Prisca and Aquila, my fellow workers in Christ Jesus, who risked their necks for my life, to whom not only I but all the churches of the Gentiles give thanks; greet also the church in their house. (Romans 16:3-5)

> The churches of Asia send greetings. Aquila and Prisca, together with the church in their house, send you hearty greetings in the Lord. (I Corinthians 16:19)

> Greet Prisca and Aquila, and the household of Onesiphorus.
> (II Timothy 4:19)

It is our loss that we do not hear more of Priscilla. That Paul and the writers thought highly of her is obvious both in the use of the affectionate name Prisca, and in placement of her name before her husband's. The most noteworthy passage, that of the Apollos story, has Priscilla as teacher, of quite a formidable student. The Staggs comment on this role:

> There is no hint here or elsewhere in Acts that a woman should be subordinate, be silent, and not teach a man.[10]

It has further been thought by a number of scholars that Priscilla is the anonymous author of the letter to the Hebrews in the New Testament.[11]

Edith Deen mentions other historical facts, not recorded in the Bible: Tertullian writes, "By the holy Prisca, the gospel is preached." One of the oldest catacombs in Rome, the Coemeterium Priscilla, is named in her honor. A church in Rome is called "Titulus St. Prisca." And a popular writing in the tenth century was called "Acts of St. Prisca."[12] Other sources say these refer to later Priscillas, perhaps the martyr St. Prisca, or a member of a senatorial family.[13] We cannot be certain these Roman titles honor the Priscilla of the New Testament, but quite possibly they do. The catacomb, especially, is a possibility because of its antiquity. And one further note: the fresco of women celebrating the Eucharist, mentioned earlier, was found in the Catacomb of Priscilla in Rome. Priscilla herself could be one of the celebrants in this ancient work.

Whatever the exact truth may be, tradition has it that Priscilla was both preacher and teacher. She further was a close companion of St. Paul, and received the honorable title, "co-worker in Christ Jesus." St. Paul gives public thanks to Priscilla and her husband, and several times mentions the church in their house. Priscilla must have been a vibrant personality, and once again we witness a woman in a leading role: preacher, companion, teacher to many.

Reading

Acts 18:2, 18, 26
Romans 16:3
I Corinthians 16:9
II Timothy 4:19

Daughters of Philip

> On the morrow we departed and came to Caesarea; and we entered the house of Philip the evangelist, who was one of the seven, and stayed with him. And he had four unmarried daughters, who prophesied. (Acts 21:8, 9)

This is the only New Testament reference we have of the daughters of Philip. Luke mentions them in passing, but in doing so, the mention assumes that women are functioning as prophets in the early church. A second document, that of Gaius in the years 198–217, refers to the "four women prophets at Hierapolis in Asia, daughters of Philip. Their grave is there, as is their father's."[14] Philip's daughters evidently gained longlasting reputation as prophets. This is further interesting when we examine the nature of worship in the early church. In a letter to the Corinthians, Paul speaks of prophecy:

> . . . he who prophesies speaks to people for their upbuilding and encouragement and consolation . . . . he who prophesies edifies the church. Now I want you all to speak in tongues, but even more to prophesy. He who prophesies is greater . . . .
>
> (I Corinthians 14:3-5)

St. Paul goes on to speak of praying with the spirit and with the mind, and singing with both spirit and mind. Worship, for the very early Christians, was quite spontaneous. A service most likely consisted of prayers, prophecy, and well-known short hymns; the worship was free-flowing, spontaneous, charismatic.[15] The Didache, an early Christian manual on morals and church practice, c. A.D. 90–110, gives instructions to those leading Eucharist; certain prayers, or thanksgivings, are quoted in full, but the author adds at the end: "In the case of prophets, however, you should let them give thanks in their own way.[16] Another version states: "But suffer the prophets to hold Eucharist as they will."[17]

Once again we have indirect reference to women as leaders in the Eucharist. Surely the daughters of Philip were charismatic preachers, and most certainly they not only "edified the church," but led the congregation in thanksgiving, as well. For they were recognized prophets, reminiscent of Miriam of old, who danced and sang and led the women in ecstatic worship.

Reading
Acts 21:8, 9

Phoebe

> I commend to you our sister Phoebe, a deaconess of the church at Cenchreae, that you may receive her in the Lord as befits the saints, and help her in whatever she may require from you, for she has been a helper of many and of myself as well.
>
> (Romans 16:1, 2)

In a letter to the Romans, Paul makes mention of a deacon named Phoebe. In actuality, this sixteenth chapter of Romans is more likely a fragment of a letter to Ephesus, for none of the people here mentioned were known to the Roman community. Phoebe, having previously been in Cenchreae, was now a messenger to Ephesus where Priscilla and Aquila were as well.

It is interesting to note that the Revised Standard and other versions translate Phoebe's title as "deaconess." The Greek word *diakonon* is used, meaning deacon. There is no term "deaconess" here or anywhere else in the New Testament.[18] We hear further mention of deacons in the account of Acts 6: the Greek believers murmur against the Jewish believers, concerning the neglect of their widows. The twelve settle the matter by summoning the community and telling them to choose seven men of good favor; these men will serve tables and function as assistants to the more notable disciples. The people are pleased, and they choose Stephen, Philip, Prochorus, Nicanor, Timon, Parmenas, and Nicolaus. The apostles pray and lay their hands on them, after which they begin functioning as deacons, or servers.

The office of deacon became more structured as years went on. In the Acts story the seven are traditionally regarded as the first deacons, but their functions are more like those of presbyters or bishops, as, for example, Stephen teaches and does not merely serve tables.[19] Yet, however the roles were intermingled at the first, the Romans passage makes clear that women as well as men were functioning as deacons in the early church.

I Timothy, written a good deal after Paul's early letters and not written by Paul himself, gives a rare detailed passage on the office of deacon:

> Deacons likewise must be serious, not doubletongued, not addicted to much wine, not greedy for gain . . . . The women likewise must be serious, no slanderers, but temperate, faithful in all things. (I Timothy 3:8-11)

In the past this passage has been explained away by saying that the women were merely the wives of deacons. Yet Pliny the Younger, writing around the beginning of the second century, also mentions Christian women who served and were called ministers or deacons.[20]

Phoebe, the deacon acclaimed by St. Paul, is a woman of high favor. Although we know little else about her, the description in Romans is complimentary: she is sister, she is saint, she helper of many, and helper of St. Paul as well. Most likely she was the bearer of the letter which Paul sent to the community at Ephesus. She would there become a deacon and leader among the people, as she was in her previous home of Cenchreae. Quite possibly Phoebe and Priscilla met in Ephesus, and there they carried out their ministries, strong women of high regard, who helped establish the growing Christian communities.

Reading
Romans 16:1
Acts 6:1–7
I Timothy 3:8–13

Euodia and Syntyche

> I entreat Euodia and I entreat Syntyche to agree in the Lord. And I ask you also, true yokefellow, help these women, for they have labored side by side with me in the gospel together with Clement and the rest of my fellow workers, whose names are in the book of life. (Philippians 4:2, 3)

Two women in the church at Philippi have been disagreeing, and Paul is concerned. He asks in his letter that these people, Euodia and Syntyche, "agree in the Lord." He further asks that they be cared for by "true yokefellow," an anonymous believer. Paul's love for the people of Philippi shows clearly in his writing:

> Therefore my friends, whom I love and long for, my joy and crown, stand firm thus in the Lord, my beloved.
> (Philippians 4:1)

These women were dear to Paul, as they worked "side by side" with him, and he wishes there to be unity in their ministry. They are "fellow workers," leaders in the community first begun by Lydia.

This passage gives us another clue into the life of the early church. Although the subject is disagreement, we see from the content that Paul considers the women equal to the men. He does not silence them or reprimand them; rather, he compliments them for their enduring work, and compares their labors with his own, with Clement's, and with others. The passage suggests, once again, that women are functioning fully as members of the community.

We have further reference to other women "co-workers" in Romans 16, the chapter which first introduces Phoebe:

> Greet Mary, who has worked hard among you . . . . Greet those workers in the Lord, Tryphaena and Tryphosa. Greet the beloved Persis, who has worked hard in the Lord . . . . Greet . . . Julia, Nereus and his sister, and Olympas, and all the saints who are with them. (Romans 16:6, 12, 15)

Mary, Tryphaena, Tryphosa, Persis, Julia, Nereus' sister, Olympas: all these women were especially greeted by Paul; many of them are referred to as "workers in the Lord." There no longer appears to be the separation of women and men as there was in the traditional Jewish community. This in itself is an amazing evolution, for neither the culture nor tradition encouraged this kind of freedom.

Reading
Philippians 4:2, 3
Romans 16:3–16

The life and ministry of Jesus, then, had great impact on the early community of followers. Women are now functioning as leaders, preachers, prophets, teachers, deacons, presbyters, and co-workers in the Lord. Foundations are shaken, customs shattered. Little wonder, then, that Acts records a Jewish complaint against Paul and Silas:

> These men who have turned the world upside down have come here also . . . . (Acts 17:6b)

Not only was their gospel revolutionary, but so also was their custom. The times were indeed changing.

But lest we think woman has been entirely freed, bonds loosed, we must examine other statements of custom and practice concerning women which appear in Paul's letters, and later letters as well. For these give us further evidence of the early church mind. While women emerge and blossom, there yet remain restriction and complaint and sometimes censure. For the early believers, nothing is as it used to be: confusion and order co-exist, and joy is countered with fear. A mix of opinions and emotions rises, as the early community tries to settle in to the new times. The writings reflect this varied sentiment. Let us, then, consider these additional passages on women.

EIGHT

Women and Saint Paul

1. Pauline passage on freedom and equality of women and men: ". . . there is neither male nor female". **2.** Pauline passage on marriage and celibacy: "It is well for a man not to touch a woman". **3.** Pauline passage on the veiling and subordination of women: ". . . woman is the glory of man". **4.** Debated Pauline passage on women keeping silence: "women . . . are not permitted to speak". **5.** Deutero-Pauline passage entreating women to "be subject to husbands". **6.** Deutero-Pauline passage describing husband as the "head" of the wife: "For the husband is the head of the wife . . . ." **7.** Deutero-Pauline passage bidding older women to be reverent and to teach younger women: "train the young women to love their husbands and children . . . ." **8.** Deutero-Pauline passage stating women are not permitted to teach: "Let a woman learn in silence with all submissiveness."

I wonder whether we must always read only one part of the evidence, following those who make Paul into the arch-chauvinist, or those who would make him a spokesman for the liberation of women, and whether, indeed, it is possible to read two such utterly opposite views from Paul's letters.[1]

Certainly Paul has often been called misogynist and chauvinist, yet scripture passages dealing with Paul and women do not warrant this strong response. Nor do they hold Paul up as feminist. They do, however, reveal a person in tension, a man with mixed notions: one who was settled and unsettled, changed and changing, just as the young church was itself. Women were, at once, free and bound in Paul's mind, and his letters reflect these opposing currents.

To better understand Paul we must keep in mind both his former life and his radical change. Before his conversion to Christianity, Paul was a Pharisee in the Judaic tradition—a member of a religious party adhering strictly to the law. In the book of Galatians Paul describes himself as a zealous guardian of tradition and fervent persecutor of early Christians:

> For you have heard of my former life in Judaism, how I persecuted the church of God violently and tried to destroy it; and I advanced in Judaism beyond many my own age among my people, so extremely zealous was I for the traditions of my fathers. (Galatians 1:13, 14)

In Philippians 3:5, 6 Paul calls himself "a Hebrew born of Hebrews," and describes his "righteousness under the law" as blameless. The tradition in Acts 22:3 tells us that Paul had been educated "at the feet of Gamaliel," a famous rabbi of the period. Acts again tells us that Paul "persecuted this Way to the death, binding and delivering to prison both men and women."

Yet Paul himself was eventually drawn to this Way, the name given to early Christians. The tradition in Acts records a dramatic conversion:

> Now as he journeyed he approached Damascus, and suddenly a light from heaven flashed about him. And he fell to the ground and heard a voice saying to him, "Saul, Saul, why do you persecute me?" (Acts 9:3, 4)

Paul's own version, written much earlier, is less spectacular:

> . . . he who had set me apart before I was born, and had called me through his grace, was pleased to reveal his Son to me . . . .
> (Galatians 1:15, 16a)

Nonetheless, the conversion is real, and Paul's life is forever changed. He sheds his life as Pharisee, becomes an ardent defender of Jesus the Christ, and begins a preaching mission to Gentiles that takes him far from home.

We see much change in all of this, yet it should not be surprising that Paul's writings contain both change and tradition. The new and the old are intricately interwoven, just as Paul himself carried both Christian and Jew in his person. St. Paul had been radicalized, yet this very radicalization brought him back, again and again, to a longing for stability and order. Thus the tension, and the conflict. Let us, then, examine a few of the passages most often noted concerning women and St. Paul.

Galatians 3:28: Freedom and Equality

> There is neither Jew nor Greek, there is neither slave nor free, there is neither male nor female; for you are all one in Christ Jesus.

St. Paul's declaration in Galatians strikes a familiar note, and we are immediately brought back to the thanksgiving included in Jewish prayers: "Praised be God that he has not created me a gentile . . . a woman . . . an ignorant man." Paul surely had this in mind when he wrote his letter to the Galatians. He takes the prayer and changes it for the new age: no longer are women, slaves, and foreigners to be separated from the community, for all are now one. Says Professor Elaine Pagels:

> Distinctions that bore religious value for Saul the Pharisee—to be Jewish, to be male, to be free—now have lost their significance as marks of spiritual superiority.[2]

Paul is concerned, in his Galatians letter, with bondage under the law as opposed to freedom in Christ. He talks at length of circumcision, advocating that it is not necessary for gentile believers, as their faith alone sustains them. In effect, he abolishes the time-honored Jewish belief that a man must be circumcised as an initiation rite into the community. The new community of Christians, he says, need no longer be constrained by such laws. The law, he continues, "was our custodian until Christ came . . . ." But we are no longer under a custodian, now that faith has come.

St. Paul is saying astounding things. He seems at once to upset the apple cart and burn the cart, so there is no going back. The law, which he used to hold in high obedience, he summarily dismisses. He even further suggests that there are no longer distinctions among Gentiles and Jews, women and men, slave and free. Yet here we must be cautious: for Paul speaks of people being one "in Christ," as they are in the spiritual order, rather than as they are in the social order. The passage most likely is not a hard case for equality, for Paul nowhere advocates that slaves should leave their masters, nor that women should disobey their husbands.

Even so, this is quite a bold statement and we might read into it more equality than at first appears. For Paul, we recall, worked very closely with many women in the early church: Lydia and her household at Philippi; Priscilla and husband Aquila, the tentmakers and preachers; Phoebe the deacon and helper of many; Euodia and Syntyche and other "co-workers in the Lord." He worked with women, stayed with women, traveled and preached in the company of women. The previous passages we examined clearly show that Paul was impressed with the work of many women; moreover, several were of personal help to Paul, and became his friends. He does not have a negative word, personally, for these co-workers in the church. Keeping this in mind, then, the passage does suggest not only a spiritual equality, but a community equality as well. Paul recognizes women as working and worshipping on an equal basis with men. For Paul, the old order is vanishing; the new has come.

I Corinthians 7: Marriage and Celibacy

> It is well for a man not to touch a woman. But because of the temptation to immorality, each man should have his own wife and each woman her own husband. (I Corinthians 7:1, 2)

Many critics of Paul do not read on in this chapter to find Paul's reasons for favoring celibacy. This opening quote has given rise to the belief that Paul was opposed to marriage because of a dislike for women. The passage must be seen in context, for in actuality, Paul is saying nothing of the kind. His concern is not so much with women or marriage, as it is with the state of celibacy. In Paul's eyes, marriage was a lesser estate in comparison with the celibate life, devoted to God.

Key to Paul's thought is his sense of urgency concerning the impending kingdom of God. In the very early days of the church, the community believed that the end of the world was fast approaching. Jesus would soon return to gather them to himself, and for this they must be prepared. St. Paul clearly subscribes to this belief and uses it as grounds for his arguments concerning marriage and slavery:

> Every one should remain in the state in which he was called.
> (I Corinthians 7:20)

> I think that in view of the present distress it is well for a person to remain as he is. (I Corinthians 7:26)

> I mean, friends, the appointed time has grown very short.
> (I Corinthians 7:29)

> For the form of this world is passing away.
> (I Corinthians 7:31b)

Paul says that slaves should remain slaves, and the unmarried should stay as they are. Where you a slave when called? he asks. Never mind. Are you bound to a wife? Do not seek to be free. Are you free from a wife? Do not seek marriage. Those who marry have worldly troubles, he says, and I would spare you that.

> From now on, let those who have wives live as though they had none, and those who mourn as though they were not mourning, and those who rejoice as though they were not rejoicing . . . .
> (I Corinthians 7:29b-30)

I want you to be free from anxieties, he goes on; the unmarried person is anxious about the affairs of the Lord, but the married person is concerned with worldly affairs, how to please husband or wife. Paul further says that if a man's "passions are strong" and he is not "behaving properly toward his betrothed," he should do as he wishes: that is, marry, for it is no sin. But, he adds, he who refrains from marriage does better.

St. Paul favors the single life, yet it is not because he feels that marriage or sex is evil. He says nothing, in this passage, to imply that woman is subordinate. On the contrary, he makes a startling claim:

> The husband should give to his wife her conjugal rights, and likewise the wife to her husband. For the wife does not rule over her own body, but the husband does; likewise the husband does not rule over his own body, but the wife does.
> (I Corinthians 7:3, 4)

This attitude was by no means widely recognized. It is also significant that Paul later addresses the wife as directly as the husband, this again being unconventional. Throughout this passage, then, duties between wife and husband are both mutual and reciprocal;[3] subordination is apparently not considered.

I Corinthians 11:2–16: Veiling and Subordination of Women

In I Corinthians 11 we first encounter Paul's masculine prejudices:

> . . . but any woman who prays or prophesies with her head uncovered dishonors her head . . . . For a man ought not to cover his head, since he is the image and glory of God; but woman is the glory of man. (I Corinthians 11:5, 7)

Paul goes on to say that man was not made for woman, but woman for man. Neither, he says, was man created for woman, but woman for man. That, he concludes, is why a woman ought to have a veil on her head, "because of the angels."

This last reference to angels is enigmatic. One interpretation suggests that angels were thought of as administering the divine order, and a woman worshipping in the presence of men shows disrespect for this order.[4] Other sources refer to the Jewish interpretation of Genesis 6:4, where angels had intercourse with women and from them giants were born.[5] The verse, then, would be a warning that women should not tempt the angels. Yet another says: no one knows what this means. Do veils ward off demonic powers? Do angels guard the created order? Do angels share in the community worship? None of these is convincing.[6]

The entire passage is indeed troublesome. Paul refers back to the rib narrative in Genesis 2 to support his argument that woman be subordinate to man. This certainly sounds quite different from his Galatians passage, or even I Corinthians 7 on marriage. Further, Paul does not make it clear why women should wear veils, the traditional sign of their subordination, especially if now women are equal to men in the congregation. He does cite what he believes to be the "natural order": the head of Christ is God, the head of man is Christ, the head of woman is man. Yet he later seems to modify this in an afterthought:

> (Nevertheless, in the Lord woman is not independent of man nor

> man of woman; for as woman was made from man, so man is now born of woman. And all things are of God.)
>
> (I Corinthians 11:11, 12)

Even with this concession, the central question remains:

> However one interprets this problematic passage, one question remains: why does Paul go back to traditional arguments for the divinely ordained . . . subordination of women?[7]

To have some insight into this we must understand the nature of the writing itself. Paul wrote his letter to the Corinthians some time after his letter to the Galatians, and he addresses different needs. In Galatians he was concerned with freedom: freedom from circumcision, freedom from the law, freedom from the "yoke of slavery." First Corinthians has an entirely different theme, that of order; the whole letter is essentially concerned with doctrinal and ethical problems that were disturbing the church at Corinth. With some situations Paul was not pleased: a man, for instance, was living with his father's wife; others, wanting to exercise their new-found freedom, were evidently practising sexual license. The city of Corinth had a particularly notorious reputation, and Paul is careful to warn his community against immorality. For Paul, the new freedom in Christ and old societal order are now in tension:

> Having proclaimed the new freedom, it seems that he finds himself appalled at the result.[8]

So Paul reacts. Having discovered this disorder and scandal in his community, his response is to revert abruptly to Jewish wisdom:[9] he appeals to authority, to the "natural order," and he warns that women must be restricted by custom and convention. It is interesting that women are the ones to bear the force of his reaction, rather than the men, who most likely were the sexual libertines. Nevertheless, he begins his reform with the lowest order, women, although his confusion concerning this is evident.

At the same time, I Corinthians 11 contains a positive statement. We are so often distracted by the subordination passages that we miss something important: Paul speaks of "any woman who prays or prophesies . . . unveiled." This assumes that women are indeed praying and prophesying within the community worship. Prophecy, as we have seen, was some form of inspired preaching, incorporated in the early liturgy. Paul may speak of subordination, but he assumes that women still take full part in public worship. Freedom and order are again in balance as the early community takes shape, evolves into an organized body.

I Corinthians 14:33b–35: Women Keeping Silence

In I Corinthians 14 we come to the most often discussed passage:

> As in all the churches of the saints, the women should keep silence . . . . for they are not permitted to speak, but should be subordinate, as even the law says. If there is anything they desire to know, let them ask their husbands at home. For it is shameful for a woman to speak in church.

The passage comes as something of a surprise, both in the context of Chapter 14 and in the mind of St. Paul, as we have seen it. Paul's strongest statement concerning subordination comes in Chapter 11 of I Corinthians, yet he nowhere suggests that women are to revert to the Jewish behavior of silence and separation. It is quite evident, in fact, that he recognizes women as praying and prophesying in worship. And further, Chapter 14 itself is a discussion of speaking in tongues and speaking in prophecy, and, we may recall, the daughters of Philip were prophets whom Paul himself visited. Chapter 14 could not be addressing just the men in the community. How, then, this discrepancy?

Several solutions have been suggested, which may be briefly summarized:

> (1) Women were allowed to prophesy publicly, but not in church.
>
> (2) Women can prophesy and pray in church, providing that they are veiled, but they are not to take part in questions or discussions afterwards.
>
> (3) I Corinthians 14:34, 35 is an interpolation, not written by Paul, and more likely a scribal gloss.[10]

Solution number one seems rather far-fetched. It is hard to suppose that men pray and prophesy in the church, and women do this elsewhere. Our former discussions of early church women would also not suggest this. Solution number two is more plausible, but it, too, has problems: if women are leaders of house churches and heads of households, it is difficult to imagine they would sit by while the men discoursed. Only if the situation in the early community were rapidly changing would this be true; that is, if they were moving back to Jewish concepts of worship. This does come, but much later.

Solution number three seems most likely, especially in the light of additional evidence. In several manuscripts, verses 34 and 35 of Chapter 14 are transposed to the end of verse 40. Further, some scholars feel the verses break the connection between 33 and 36. It is possible, say some, that this passage is a gloss by a scribal hand, introduced into the letter at a later point. Further, the verses highly resemble I Timothy 2:11, 12, a much later passage not written by St. Paul. And finally, it is argued, Paul would hardly appeal to the Torah in the section "even as the law says." This in itself would be quite surprising, if indeed Paul wrote it, and in addition it is unclear what "law" this refers to.[11]

It seems fair, then, to give Paul the benefit of the doubt in this particular passage, yet we are still left wondering. What, then, is Paul's attitude as we have seen it in his work with women and in his letters to the churches of Galatia and Corinth? The evidence seems quite mixed, but more positive than not. On the one hand we have Paul's high regard for his women companions: Lydia, Priscilla, Phoebe, Euodia, Syntyche, and others. He appears to admire these people and their work, and he nowhere indicates that they should abandon their teaching, preaching, serving, and leading for a lesser role of subservience and silence.

Yet Corinthians gives us contradictory evidence, even dismissing the I Corinthians 14:34, 35 passage. We have to assume that St. Paul acted on a vision, that of Galatians 3:28, and as the vision became at times improbable, he returned to what he knew: Jewish custom and Jewish order. For Paul was not only a Christian, but centuries of Jew. The experience of the risen Lord has shaken and shattered him, yet as he grew away from the charisma and ecstasy of the conversion, and as Jesus had yet to return, Paul turned once again to the order and stability of things. But he never quite returned; his favorable attitude toward women is quite arresting, considering his background, and this is for us to remember. Women were helping to bring in the imminent kingdom of God, and it was this, in Paul's mind, that held greatest importance.

Household Codes in Deutero-Pauline Letters

A few remaining passages regarding women in early times need to be considered. Other writings are sometimes quoted in reference to Paul and women, when most likely these were written by others. Colossians, Ephesians, and the Pastoral Letters (I Timothy, II Timothy, Titus) are thought to be works of the Pauline school, rather than written by Paul himself. The dates of these vary, Colossians and Ephesians probably dating from the seventies or eighties of the first century; the Pastorals at least a generation later, reflecting the concerns of the church at the beginning of the second century.[12] The letters all claim to be written by Paul, but there was a widespread custom of pseudonymous authorship which allowed others to write in the name of one more notable. In many instances the distinctions are accounted for by differences in vocabulary, style, thought, and dating.[13]

In *The Gnostic Gospels*, Elaine Pagels comments on these passages:

> By the year 200, the majority of Christian communities endorsed as canonical the pseudo-Pauline letter of Timothy, which stresses (and exaggerates) the antifeminist element in Paul's views . . . . Orthodox Christians also accepted as Pauline the letters to the Colossians and to the Ephesians, which order that women "be subject in everything to their husbands."[14]

The material in these writings is generally known as the Domestic Code, or the Household Code. These are comprised of class lists and corresponding duties—masters, servants, husbands, wives, parents, children; they are a characteristic feature of the post-apostolic letters and do not appear in the authentic writings of Paul. Some feel these household codes were older than Paul, and came first from fourth century B.C. Stoicism by the way of Hellenistic Christianity.[15] Others feel the codes were developed to meet the needs for order within the churches, and the domestic and civil structures of society.[16] The code most probably was adapted from an earlier culture and Christianized for the purposes of the early community, as it grew and became ordered.

Let us, then, consider briefly a few of these Household Codes, as they appear in the deutero-Pauline letters:

Colossians

> Wives, be subject to your husbands, as it is fitting in the Lord.
> (Colossians 3:18)

Colossians 3:18–4:1 speaks of duties concerning wives and husbands, children and parents, slaves and masters. Wives are to be subject to husbands, and husbands are to love wives. Children are to obey parents "in everything," and fathers are not to provoke children. Slaves are to obey their "earthly masters," and masters are to treat slaves justly and fairly.

Prior to this Household Code, Colossians 3:11 reflects a similarity to Galatians 3:28, only now the equality of female and male is absent:

> Here there cannot be Greek or Jew, circumcised and uncircumcised, barbarian, Scythian, slave, free man, but Christ is all, and in all.

In her book *The Lady was a Bishop,* Joan Morris comments that the "male and female" omitted from this passage does appear in some Greek and Old Latin manuscripts. According to Morris, the omission in our present Colossians text is the work of an antifeminist scribe.[17]

The omittance of the "male and female" reference is telling: women are moving away from freedom, into order. The writers of the early church are beginning to stabilize the charismatic community, and the recall of the subordination of women is reflected in the Code.

Ephesians

> Wives, be subject to your husbands, as to the Lord. For the husband is the head of the wife as Christ is the head of the church, his body . . . . As the church is subject to Christ, so let wives also be subject in everything to their husbands.
> (Ephesians 5:22–24)

Ephesians 5:22–6:9 follows the basic outline of the Code: wives are to be subject to husbands, children to parents, slaves to masters. The letter to the Ephesians is considered later than Colossians, and the writer's dependence on Colossians is evident. The instructions in Ephesians become more elaborate, and thus we have a detailed metaphor of husband, wife, Christ, and church:

> Husbands, love your wives as Christ loved the church and gave himself up for her, that he might sanctify her, having cleansed her . . . . that she might be holy and without blemish.
>
> (Ephesians 5:25–27)

The implication stands that if husbands love wives, the wives, also, will be cleansed. It is true that the Household Codes somewhat modify and soften traditional Jewish subordination, in that both wives and husbands are equally addressed and equally responsible in marriage, yet it is startling to see the age-old theme, however cloaked, that woman is unclean. Once again women are subject and subordinate, and the "new freedom in Christ" appears to be fast fading.

Titus

> Bid the older women likewise to be reverent in behavior, not to be slanderers or slaves to drink; they are to teach what is good, and so train the young women to love their husbands and children, to be sensible, chaste, domestic, kind, and submissive to their husbands . . . . (Titus 2:3–5)

It is likely that Titus was written earlier than I Timothy, so we shall consider this passage first.[18] The Pastoral Letters, that is, I and II Timothy and Titus, were written some time after Colossians and Ephesians, and begin to reflect church order of the second century. In Titus 2:1–10 we see the old cultural Household Code adapted for the church community: Titus speaks of older men, older women, young women, young men, and slaves. Older men in the Christian community are to be temperate, serious, sensible, and sound; older women are to be reverent in behavior and teachers of younger women. Young women are to be sensible, chaste, domestic, kind, and submissive; young men are to control themselves. Slaves are to be submissive to their masters.

In the Household Code of Titus there can be no doubt that woman is ascribed a domestic role. Older women can teach younger women, but only the affairs of the family. Young women are only mentioned in relation to husband and children. The reason for proper behavior is stated: ". . . that the word of God may not be discredited." (2:5b) The Household Code, as we can see, was adapted for both order within the community, and for the church's credibility to the outside world. Behind the Code lies a strong motive for satisfying the requirements of society.[19] The subordinate role again stands clear, as the church moves into the second century.

I Timothy

> Let a woman learn in silence with all submissiveness. I permit no woman to teach or to have authority over men; she is to keep silent. For Adam was formed first, then Eve; and Adam was not deceived, but the woman was deceived and became a transgressor. Yet woman will be saved through bearing children, if she continues in faith and love and holiness, with modesty.
> (I Timothy 2:11–15)

The entire letter of I Timothy is mostly Household Code, modified for the Christian community. The writer makes mention of rulers, men, women, bishops, deacons, widows, and slaves. Chapter 2:1–15 is concerned with the regulation of worship. The writer asks that "supplications, prayers, intercessions, and thanksgivings" be made for kings and all in high positions, "that we may lead a quiet and peaceable life, godly and respectful in every way." He goes on to request that in every place men should pray, "lifting holy hands without anger or quarreling." The women, he says, should adorn themselves modestly and sensibly: not with braided hair or gold or pearls or costly attire. And then comes the final directive: women are to be silent, be submissive, and not teach. They can hold no authority over men. The writer's reasons come from the rib narrative; first Adam, then Eve, and the woman was the transgressor. Yet, the writer concludes, woman may be saved through bearing children.

One wonders what was occuring in this community. The writer is at pains to speak of "living peaceably," without anger or quarreling. The women are to be modestly attired (cf. a similar passage in I Peter 3:1–7). But above all, the women are to be silent. All of these statements presuppose that the community was divided over something, and women were, for this writer, a major source of concern. Apparently women were still involved, at the beginning of the second century, in worship, whether it be preaching, prophesying, or liturgical functioning. But order must be maintained at all cost, and the writer appeals to the rib narrative for his authority, and further, attributes the letter to Paul. Say the Staggs:

> There can be no doubt as to the writer's commitment to marriage and homemaking as the proper vocation for women.[20]

* * *

The Household Code as seen in these passages indicates the direction of the church: from people of freedom to people of stability. Spontaneity is gone; order takes its place. From the fifties and sixties on a change begins, as evidenced in Paul's letter to the unruly Corinthians. The community grows away from the great mandate of Galatians to the cautious peace of Timothy. Paul himself remains an extraordinary champion of freedom, although he, too, modifies his views. According to tradition, Paul dies in Rome c. 58–60 A.D. The early Christians continue on, becoming less of a community and more an organized, although by no means established, church.

As time went on and problems arose, new structures and limitations formed. Beginning with Colossians and moving through the Pastoral Letters, it becomes evident that order is once again recalled, and woman is again viewed with some distrust; she is instructed to be obedient, and to be quiet. The rib narrative of the creation story seems to underlie many of the Household Codes, and woman suffers the consequence.

Jesus is gone. Paul is gone. And with them goes, apparently, the other story of creation, that of woman and man being created equally, in the image and likeness of God.

NINE

Women and the Christian Fathers

> It is not permitted to a woman to speak in the church; but neither (is it permitted her) to teach, nor to baptize, nor to offer [the eucharist], nor to claim to herself a lot in any manly function, not to say (in any) sacerdotal office.
>
> (Tertullian, A.D. 204 On the Veiling of Virgins)

Elaine Pagels states that by the year 200, there is no evidence for women taking prophetic, priestly, and episcopal roles among orthodox churches. In the middle of the second century women and men no longer sat together for worship; instead, they were separated, adopting the synagogue custom. By the end of the second century, Pagels continues, women's participation in worship was explicitly condemned: groups in which women held leadership were branded as heretical.[1]

What are we to make of this? And what are we to make of the extreme statements of the church Fathers, concerning women? Leonard Swidler, in his book *Biblical Affirmations of Woman*, has compiled sayings of the Greek and Latin Fathers of later centuries, and we offer these, in part, for consideration:

Greek Fathers[2]

> His beard, then, is the badge of a man and shows him unmistaka-

bly to be a man. It is older than Eve and is the symbol of the stronger nature . . . . His characteristic is action; hers, passivity . . . . the male is hairier and more warm-blooded than the female; the uncastrated, than the castrated; the mature, than the immature. [in praise of the beard]

(Clement of Alexandria A.D. 150–215)

What is seen with the eyes of the creator is masculine, and not feminine, for God does not stoop to look upon what is feminine and of the flesh. (Origen A.D. 185–254)

The one who is not entirely pure in soul and body must be stopped from entering the Holy of Holies. (concerning menstruating women) (Dionysius the Great A.D. 190-264)

For the female sex is easily seduced, weak, and without much understanding. The devil seeks to vomit out this disorder through women . . . . We wish to apply masculine reasoning and destroy the folly of these women. (attacking a group which praised Mary as divinely honored) (Epiphanius A.D. 315-403)

Should you reflect about what is contained in beautiful eyes, in a straight nose, in a mouth, in cheeks, you will see that bodily beauty is only a white-washed tomb, for inside it is full of filth. (writing to a monk considering marriage)

(John Chrysostom A.D. 347–407)

Somehow the woman, or rather, the female sex as a whole, is slow in comprehension. (explaining Mary Magdalene's failure to recognize Jesus after the resurrection)

(Cyril of Alexandria A.D. 376–444)

These statements are incredible. They appear to be bitter, acrid, and arrogant. But more than this, we would detect a subtle fear underlying the vendettas and accusations. Again we raise the questions: What is there to fear? What inherent power does woman hold, even in her supposed weakness?

If we examine these statements more closely, we see the repetition of particular themes: the condemnation of Eve, the condemnation of the flesh, the condemnation of blood. We would translate these into fear of Eve, fear of flesh, fear of blood. The writers seem to assume the Yahwist creation story takes precedence over the Priestly account, for woman being made in the image of God is nowhere considered.

Instead she is Eve: the weak, the seduced, the dull. She is impure, unclean, and filthy. Her very presence suggests the flesh, and therefore she is to be avoided. Here again we would question the writers' underlying assumptions: where did this dualism come from? Flesh and sin; spirit and purity. This seems to be a Greek notion that the Fathers interpolated and adapted into the Christian view of woman. Perhaps, too, they misinterpreted St. Paul; in his zeal to watch for the coming kingdom, Paul regarded relations between women and men as distracting and unnecessary. Yet interpreted in later centuries, "it is better not to touch a woman" could become just that. One of the Latin Fathers does make reference to this:

> If it is good not to touch a woman, then it is bad to touch a woman always and in every case.[3] (Jerome A.D. 342–420)

Some of the Fathers took their asceticism to extremes: Origen castrated himself. Others despised marriage and celebrated the monastic life.[4] Still others viciously attacked "heretical" orders which continued to allow the participation of women:

> And the women of these heretics, how wanton they are! For they are bold enough to teach, to dispute, to enact exorcisims, to undertake cures—maybe even to baptize.[5]
>
> (Tertullian A.D. 160–225)

The views of Jerome and Tertullian were shared by many other of the Latin Fathers; women were mostly valued as virgins, widows, and ascetics. Beyond that, the negative attitude prevailed.

Latin Fathers[6]

> You are the devil's gateway; you are the unsealer of that (forbidden) tree: you are the first deserter of the divine law: you are she who persuaded him whom the devil was not valiant enough to attack. You destroyed so easily God's image, man. (writing to Christian women concerning their dress)
>
> (Tertullian A.D. 160–225)

> Whoever does not believe is a woman, and she is still addressed with her physical sexual designation; for the woman who believes is elevated to male completeness and to a measure of the stature of the fullness of Christ; then she no longer bears the worldly name of her physical sex . . . . (Ambrose A.D. 339–397)

> . . . the woman is inferior to man, for she is part of him, because the man is the origin of woman; from that and on account of that the woman is subject to the man, in that she is under his command . . . . The man is created in the image of God, but not the woman. (commenting on I Corinthians 11)
>
> ("Ambrosiaster": pseudo-Ambrose)

> What do these wretched sin-laden hussies want! . . . Simon Magus founded a heretical sect with the support of the harlot Helena. Nicholas of Antioch, the contriver of everything filthy, directed women's groups . . . . Apelles had Philomena as companion for his teaching. Montanus, the proclaimer of the spirit of impurity, first used Prisca and Maximilla, noble and rich women, to seduce many communities by gold . . . . (Jerome A.D. 342-420)

> I feel that nothing so casts down the manly mind from its height as the fondling of a woman . . . . (Augustine A.D. 354–430)

> Flesh stands for woman, because she was made out of a rib . . . . Flesh thus stands for the wife, as sometimes also spirit for the husband. (Augustine)

> In Holy Scripture [the word] "woman" stands either for the female sex (Gal. 4:4) or for weakness, as it is said: A man's spite is preferable to a woman's kindness (Sir. 42:14). For every man is called strong and clear of thought, but woman is looked upon as a weak or muddled spirit . . . .
>
> (Gregory the Great A.D. 540–604)

Again the themes reoccur, with startling regularity: woman is flesh and therefore evil; she is created from the rib of man; she is not created in the image of God. She is "the devil's gateway" and "sin-laden hussy." She is also muddled, wretched, and incomplete. The Latin Fathers, it seemed, placed great value on the woman who "became like a man," that is, one who followed a life of extreme asceticism. The Fathers further regarded marriage as having two ends: to produce offspring and to avoid fornication.[7]

In his compilation of sayings, Swidler makes note that some of the Fathers had "severe difficulties" with their sexuality. Jerome had "wild sexual fantasies"; Augustine had a common-law wife, a mistress, and a difficult relationship with his mother.[8] Whatever the psychological make-up of these people, one thing is clear: they had lost the vision of the early church. Quite simply, they had lost sight of Jesus.

Swidler further relates a story concerning one of the Greek Fathers, Cyril of Alexandria: When Cyril became bishop at Alexandria, the most celebrated non-Christian mathematician and philosopher of the Alexandrian Neoplatonic school was a woman, Hypatia. Hypatia was known for her "great eloquence, rare modesty, and beauty;" she attracted many students and was in opposition to Cyril, an authoritarian. One day Christian monks "dragged her from her chariot into a Christian church, stripped her naked, cut her throat, and burned her piecemeal." Cyril was deeply complicit, indirectly if not directly.[9]

Stories like this should make us weep. For what happened to Hypatia was symbolically happening to women of the church: woman was stripped, naked; she was humiliated, scorned, and condemned. She alone carried the burden of sin; she alone bore a tarnished image. Woman was, from the second century on, back where she began.

What happened? Why did people lose sight of the vision and teaching of Jesus? Why was woman so despised? There are no easy answers. It may be that we do not yet have the answers at all. We can, however, give some reasons for these changes, as seen from sundry points of view. We offer, then, for consideration, the thinking of several contemporaries previously quoted.

In a discussion with Elaine Pagels concerning her work *The Gnostic Gospels*, a professor of classics raises the question: Is the antiwoman bias of the orthodox Christian church a reaction to gnostic feminism? Or was it just a natural development from Judaism? The questioner continues: Mary Magdalene may or may not have been a whore, but she is depicted as a reformed whore in orthodox Christianity, while in Gnostic sources she is depicted as a seer and a prophet. Pagels responds: I don't think anybody knows the answer to that. I wish we did. . . . we just don't know why it happened. I am puzzled by it.[10]

In her book Pagels reviews this question. It is clear, she says, that by the year 200 things had changed. Both orthodox and gnostic texts suggest that the question of women was "explosively controversial." She notes that the *Gospel of Philip*, the *Dialogue of the Savior*, and the *Gospel of Mary*, all gnostic texts and therefore not included in the New Testament canon, balance heavily in favor of woman. Mary Magdalene is described as Jesus' "most intimate companion, and symbol of divine wisdom." She is praised above male disciples as "a woman who knew the All." She further challenges leaders of the orthodox community, including Peter. In these texts Jesus sides with Mary, rebuking criticism against her.

Orthodox Christians, continues Pagels, retaliated with alleged "apostolic" letters making the opposite point. Examples of these are the pseudo-Pauline letters of I and II Timothy, Colossians, Ephesians, and Titus. Attributing the letters to Paul, the writers insist that women be subordinate to men.

Two patterns emerge then, says Pagels. Many gnostic Christians correlate their description of God in both masculine and feminine terms, with a complimentary description of human nature. Most often they refer to the creation account of Genesis 1. The orthodox pattern, however, is strikingly different. It describes God in exclusively masculine terms, and typically refers to Genesis 2, the Eve/Adam story.[11]

Pagels' theory, at its simplest, contends that from the second century on, ideas which tended to oppose or impede the institutional church came to be called heretical, while ideas which implicity supported the development of the institutional church came to be called orthodox.[12] Gnosticism, then, was called heresy, and participating women were called heretics. One side lost, one side won: woman lost, and the church moved on.

Leonard Swidler also raises the question of women and the growing church:

> Why, with such a clear difference in attitude expressed by Jesus and by some of the Pauline writings, did Christianity's choice go not to Jesus but to the negative Pauline and deutero-Pauline writings?

He goes on to cite several possible reasons. First, the rigid patriarchal system, which Jesus did his best to dismantle, apparently was so pervasive that many Christians "automatically gravitated toward the most restrictive, subordinationist passages of the New Testament." Christianity became intent on differentiating itself from the pagan world, a world which included a relatively high status for women.

Secondly, as long as the *parousia*, the second coming of Christ, was expected momentarily, there was little need to develop organized structures. But as time went on and the hope of the coming faded, the need for order prevailed. Christians began to pattern themselves after familiar societal structures. In the Greco-Roman society, women were almost entirely excluded from political life, and as the church began to model civil authority, women were excluded here also.

Third, the Greek notion of dualism prevailed: matter is evil; spirit is good. Woman became identified with the flesh, and man, with the spirit. Asceticism became the highest ideal.

Fourth, Christians in the Greco-Roman world competed with the worship of the Goddess, especially the cult of Isis, venerated under various names: Demeter, Athena, Venus, Ceres. Although the Isis cult did not promote sexual excesses of promiscuity, it was widely rumored as doing so, and thus the women priests of Isis were negatively received. The Goddess was an effective rival to early Christianity from the second century on; public worship of the Isis cult remained until 560 A.D.

According to Swidler, woman, then, was defeated by the entrenched patriarchal system, by political institution, by prevailing philosophy, and by a deep mistrust of woman as God. All these contributed to her demise. There is a special irony, says Swidler, in that by turning toward the subordination of women, Christianity turned away from its Jewish founder Jesus, and his feminist attitude.[13]

Other writers make mention of the disappearance of women preachers and teachers, and of the lack of women priests in ancient Israel. Elisabeth Tetlow comments that by the end of the first century, the ministry of preaching and teaching was absorbed by the office of presbyter, or priest. The office of presbyter then merged with office of bishop, and this office eventually became identified with the Old Testament model of levitical high priesthood. Women were therefore excluded from both offices, and from preaching. In the second century, the exclusively male office of levitical priest became the standard for Christian ministry.[14]

Evelyn and Frank Stagg cite possible reasons for there being no women priests in Israel: there were priestesses alongside priests in the ancient pagan world; the exclusion of women priests in Israel may have been due to the long struggle between Yahwism and the fertility religions. The presence of sacred prostitutes in the fertility cults could have prejudiced the case for priestesses in the worship of Yahweh. Further, women were "unclean" during menstruation and therefore could not participate in the holy. Shrines and altars would not tolerate "defilement."[15] Women priests, therefore, were never recognized in Israel, and later would not be recognized in the early church as it began to define and limit its order. Former roles of women melted into the priestly office; when the offices began to shape and become institution, woman was excluded.

Gerhard Kittel makes mention of women deacons: with the passage of time, he says, these women clergy were more and more restricted to activity in divine service, assistance at the baptism of women, visitation of women, the bringing of the elements for the Lord's supper. In both East and West, he continues, the decisions against women exercising priestly functions became increasingly strict. The history of the ministry of women finally ended in the convent; the title of "deaconess" was borne by the abbess in the early Middle Ages.[16] We have further evidence of the decline of women deacons from Church Council statements:

> Let no one proceed to the ordination of deaconesses anymore.
>
> Council of Orange (A.D. 441), Canon 26

> We abrogate completely in the entire kingdom the consecration of widows who are named deaconesses.
>
> Council of Epaon (A.D. 517), Canon 21

> No longer shall the blessing of women deaconesses be given, because of the weakness of the sex.
>
> Council of Orleans II (A.D. 533)[17]

That all this happened is clear, but why it happened remains clouded.

Perhaps Rosemary Ruether touches closest to the truth when she considers "Why Males Fear Women Priests." The priest, she says, mediates the enfleshed Word, the *body* of Christ. The Christ who feeds us with his body is imaged, in long traditions of mysticism and piety, as a mother feeding us with milk from his breasts. Ruether continues: the roles of feeding, washing, and serving of the priest at the altar suggest more what mothers do than what fathers do. Woman as priest reveals the "enfleshed and maternal imagery" of the role and thus much more directly challenges it as a male role. Perhaps it is this maternal sacrality, she concludes, that caused males to "fence the sanctuary" and to rid it of its supposed impurity.[18]

Ruether's argument is highly plausible. To cite a quite personal example, when this writer was first a deacon, setting up numerous chalices and patens on an altar, one man was heard to say: "You can tell that gal has been in the kitchen before!" At first this seemed an insult, but over the years it transformed to high compliment. For perhaps what the man saw in a woman deacon was what the very early church saw in its women leaders: people who fit a function. People who knew how to clean and wash and feed and teach and hold, because they did it naturally, without thought, like breathing. Quite possibly there is something about a woman at the altar that is akin to being in the kitchen: she does it naturally, and often with an unsurpassed grace.

If this be true, perhaps we have a clue to the vehement reaction against women after the first century. For woman as Goddess, or woman imaging Mother, woman simply fulfilling a quite natural role, would indeed be a fearful and awesome thing to those not possessing that kind of elemental power. Woman was therefore attacked and belittled and suppressed: held down. She became, once again, the person seated behind the screen, hidden by the veil, the nameless one.

Again, it is difficult to know what is true. The foregoing reasons for loss of woman's leadership in the second century church are not answers: they are speculation, guess, assumption. We simply do not know what happened. It is, as Pagels says, a puzzle, a great mystery. We do know that something went amiss, that women no longer taught and preached and prophesied and presided. Instead, they became virgins or martyrs or honored widows; they instructed the young and kept their silence. We do know that the vision of Jesus was lost, and that St. Paul's quite startling affirmation of "neither male nor female" lost its electric intent. We further know that the wonderful creation story of woman and man in the image of God, equally born, was also lost.

And finally, we know that something about all this does not ring high and true, and this is our work to inherit. We can only trust that the mystery will be made clear, as we go along, and we can also trust that there are many, many ancestors moving with us. For now we see through a glass darkly, says St. Paul, but then we shall see, face to face.

EPILOGUE

After one particularly disturbing session, while teaching this series, a young woman said to me: What I want to know is, does this stuff ever make you angry? or do you just laugh it off? What do you do with your anger? She was asking, of course, for herself, but I answered anyway. Well I'm writing a book, I said. And yes it makes me angry, but I've been doing this for a long time. She then said she knew how her anger would come out: it would be in the supper cheese sandwiches for her husband and children. Slapped right into the sandwiches, she said, and there's nothing I can do about it. We then, the entire class, talked of what to do about it. We talked about Jesus and his anger, and we talked about how he saw through anger, to the other side. He saw the people and had compassion on them, for they were like sheep, without a shepherd. Compassion: to have the bowels ache. Possibly God calls us both to the anger and through it to the compassion on the other side. There are many of us, writers and women and men and narrators all, who are like sheep without a shepherd. Keep your eye on the vision, I said to the class. Keep your eye on Jesus, for he carries the hope.

The question they didn't ask me is the one that haunts, and the one that underlies many of the others: Why do you stay in the Church? Why do you keep on, after all the name-calling and the accusation, and the blinding, creeping prejudice? Why should any of us stay in the Church, with this kind of history behind us, and present with us?

Long ago, in seminary, a friend said to me that all of us there were broken people. And I see it still. On Sunday morning, when I stand in front, watching people come for bread and wine, I see that we are all very broken people. We all kneel, heads bowed, and it is clear we are hurt, broken, in many ways. Perhaps this is why many of us remain in the Church, long after we have lost patience with its theology, language, and practice. For we come to the altar for healing, to the holy place where God lives, and where God's people gather. We come because our families have come, and our families' families have come, and because our foremothers and forefathers for centuries have come. We come in hope and in love and in confidence that things will not always be the same: for God is with us, has come among us, and we have seen the glory.

FOOTNOTES

Introduction

1. Gerhard Von Rad, *Genesis* (Philadelphia: The Westminster Press, 1976), p. 25.
2. Ibid., p. 57.
3. Ibid., p. 25.

Chapter one

1. Evelyn and Frank Stagg, *Woman in the World of Jesus* (Philadelphia: The Westminster Press, 1978), p. 23.
2. Gerhard Kittel, ed., *Theological Dictionary of the New Testament*, vol. 1, (Grand Rapids, Mich.: Wm. B. Eerdmans Publishing Co., 1972), p. 781.
3. Stagg, *Woman*, p. 24.
4. Elizabeth Cady Stanton, ed., *The Woman's Bible* (Seattle, Wash.: Seattle Coalition Task Force on Women and Religion, 1974), p. 73.
5. Gerhard Von Rad, *Genesis* (Philadelphia: The Westminster Press, 1976), pp. 221, 223.
6. Stanton, *Woman's Bible*, pp. 46.
7. Ibid., pp. 62, 63.
8. Von Rad, *Genesis*, p. 331.
9. *The Oxford Annotated Bible* (RSV), (New York, Oxford University Press, 1973), footnotes, pp. 43, 44.
10. Stanton, *Woman's Bible*, p. 67.
11. Merlin Stone, *When God Was a Woman* (New York: Harcourt Brace Jovanovich, 1976), p. 54.
12. Von Rad, *Genesis*, p. 360.
13. Ibid, p. 359.

Chapter two

1. Edith Deen, *All of the Women of the Bible* (New York: Harper and Row, 1955), p. 45.

2. Gerhard Von Rad, *Genesis* (Philadelphia: The Westminster Press, 1976), p. 366.

3. *The Oxford Annotated Bible* (RSV) (New York: Oxford University Press, 1973), footnotes, p. 87.

4. Ibid., footnotes, p. 179.

5. Elizabeth Cady Stanton, ed., *The Woman's Bible* (Seattle, Wash.: Seattle Coalition Task Force on Women and Religion, 1974), p. 102.

6. Deen, *All of the Women*, pp. 60, 61.

7. Stanton, *Woman's Bible*, p. 124.

Chapter three

1. Edith Deen, *All of the Women of the Bible* (New York: Harper and Row, 1955), p. 67.

2. Elizabeth Cady Stanton, ed., *The Woman's Bible* (Seattle, Wash.: Seattle Coalition Task Force on Women and Religion, 1974), part II, p. 20.

3. Ibid., pp. 25–26.

4. Deen, *All of the Women*, p. 78.

Chapter four

1. Edith Deen, *All of the Women of the Bible* (New York: Harper and Row, 1955), pp. 106, 107.

2. Ibid., p. 112.

Chapter five

1. Edith Deen, *All of the Women of the Bible* (New York: Harper and Row, 1955), p. 126.

2. Rosemary Ruether, "Mary—The Feminine Face of the Church," *Enquiry*, vol. 9, no. 2 (December 1976–February 1977), pp. 4, 5.

3. Merlin Stone, *When God Was a Woman* (New York: The Dial Press, 1976), pp. xii–xiii.

4. George Arthur Buttrick, ed., *The Interpreter's Dictionary of the Bible*, vol. 1 (Nashville, Tenn.: Abingdon Press, 1962), p. 251.

5. Deen, *All of the Women*, pp. 140–141.

6. Stanton, *The Woman's Bible*, part II, p. 83.

Chapter six

1. Leonard Swidler, "Jesus was a Feminist," p. 1.

2. Gerhard Kittel, ed., *Theological Dictionary of the New Testament*, vol. 1 (Grand Rapids, Mich.: Wm. B. Eerdmans Publishing Co., 1972), p. 781.

3. Swidler, "Feminist," pp. 1, 2.

4. Reginald H. Fuller, *A Critical Introduction to the New Testament* (London: Duckworth, 1971), p. 93.

5. Ibid., p. 95.

6. Swidler, "Feminist," p. 3.

7. Evelyn and Frank Stagg, *Woman in the World of Jesus* (Philadelphia: The Westminster Press, 1978), p. 114.

8. Ibid., p. 114.

9. Kittel, *Theological Dictionary*, p. 781.

10. Stagg, *Woman*, p. 106.

11. Elaine Pagels, *The Gnostic Gospels* (New York: Random House, 1979), p. xv.

12. Kittel, *Theological Dictionary*, p. 785.

Chapter seven

1. Gerhard Kittel, ed., *Theological Dictionary of the New Testament*, vol. 1 (Grand Rapids, Mich.: Wm. B. Eerdmans Publishing Co., 1972), p. 785.

2. Evelyn and Frank Stagg, *Woman in the World of Jesus* (Philadelphia: The Westminster Press, 1978), p. 206.

3. Ibid., p. 227.

4. Elisabeth M. Tetlow, *Women and Ministry in the New Testament* (New York: Paulist Press, 1980), p. 108.

5. Leonard Swidler, *Biblical Affirmations of Woman* (Philadelphia: The Westminster Press, 1979), pp. 296–297.

6. Josef A. Jungmann, *The Early Liturgy* (Notre Dame, Ind.: University of Notre Dame Press, 1959), p. 31.

7. Ibid., p. 31.

8. Dorothy Irvin, "Archaeology Supports Women's Ordination," in *The Witness*, (vol. 63, no. 2, February 1980), p. 5.

9. Ibid., p. 6.

10. Stagg, *Woman*, p. 231.

11. Swidler, *Biblical Affirmations*, p. 298.

12. Edith Deen, *All of the Women of the Bible* (New York: Harper and Row, 1955), p. 229.

13. F. L. Cross, ed., *The Oxford Dictionary of the Christian Church* (Oxford University Press, 1974, 2nd ed.), "Priscilla, St.," p. 1126.

14. Swidler, *Biblical Affirmations*, p. 302.

15. Charles P. Price, Professor of Systematic Theology, The Virginia Theological Seminary.

16. Cyril C. Richardson, ed., *Early Christian Fathers* (The Macmillan Company, 1970), "The Didache," p. 176.

17. T. E. Page and W. H. D. Rouse, eds., *The Apostolic Fathers*, vol. I (London: William Heinemann, 1912), "The Didache," p. 325.

18. Stagg, *Woman*, p. 180.

19. *The Oxford Annotated Bible* (RSV) (New York: Oxford University Press, 1973), footnotes, "Choice of the Seven," p. 1326.

20. Tetlow, *Women and Ministry*, p. 128.

Chapter eight

1. Elaine Pagels, "Paul and Women: A Response to Recent Discussion." *Journal of the American Academy of Religion*, XLII (1974), p. 544.

2. Ibid., p. 540.

3. Evelyn and Frank Stagg, *Woman in the World of Jesus* (Philadelphia: The Westminster Press, 1978) p. 170.

4. *The Oxford Annotated Bible* (RSV) (New York: Oxford University Press, 1973), footnotes, p. 1390.

5. Stagg. *Woman*, p. 176.

6. Wayne A. Meeks, ed., *The Writings of St, Paul* (New York: W. W. Norton & Co., 1972), note 5, p. 38.

7. Pagels, "*Paul and Women*," p. 544.

8. Ibid., p. 546.

9. Ibid., p. 544.

10. D. E. H. Whiteley, *The Theology of St. Paul* (Philadelphia: Fortress Press, 1972), pp. 224–225.

11. Ibid., p. 224. Stagg, *Woman*, pp. 178–179.

12. Norman Perrin, *The New Testament: An Introduction* (New York: Harcourt Brace Jovanovich, 1974), p. 119.

13. *The Oxford Annotated Bible*, introduction to I Timothy, p. 1440; introduction to II Peter, p. 1480.

14. Elaine Pagels, *The Gnostic Gospels* (New York: Random House, 1979), p. 63.

15. Reginald H. Fuller, *A Critical Introduction to the New Testament* (London: Duckworth, 1971), pp. 18, 19, 64.

16. Stagg. *Woman*, p. 187.

17. Joan Morris, *The Lady was a Bishop* (New York: The Macmillan Co., 1973), pp. 122, 123.

18. Perrin, *New Testament*, pp. 267–268.

19. Stagg, *Woman*, pp. 198–199.

20. Ibid., p. 201.

Chapter nine

1. Elaine Pagels, *The Gnostic Gospels* (New York: Random House, 1979), pp. 61, 63.
2. Leonard Swidler, *Biblical Affirmations of Woman* (Philadelphia: The Westminster Press, 1979), pp. 342–344.
3. Ibid., p. 348.
4. Ibid, pp. 342, 343.
5. Roger Gryson, *The Ministry of Women in the Early Church* (Collegeville, Minn.: The Liturgical Press, 1976), p. 17.
6. Swidler, *Biblical Affirmations*, pp. 346–351.
7. Ibid., pp. 347, 348.
8. Ibid., pp. 347–349.
9. Ibid., p. 345.
10. Elaine Pagels, "Gnostic Texts Revive Ancient Controversies," *The Center Magazine* (September/October 1980), p. 58.
11. Pagels, *Gnostic Gospels*, pp. 64–66.
12. Pagels, "Gnostic Texts," p. 56.
13. Swidler, *Biblical Affirmations*, pp. 354–356.
14. Elizabeth M. Tetlow, *Women and Ministry in the New Testament* (New York: Paulist Press, 1980) pp. 127, 129.
15. Stagg, *Woman*, pp. 29–32.
16. Gerhard Kittel, ed., Theological Dictionary of the New Testament, vol. 1 (Grand Rapids, Mich.: Wm. B. Eerdmans Publishing Co., 1972) p. 789.
17. Swidler, *Biblical Affirmations*, p. 314.
18. Rosemary Ruether, "Why Males Fear Women Priests," *The Witness* (vol. 63, no. 7, July 1980), p. 21.

SUGGESTIONS FOR FURTHER READING

Butterick, George Arthur, ed., *The Interpreter's Dictionary of the Bible*, Vol. 1. Nashville, Tenn.: Abingdon Press, 1962

Cross, F.L., ed., *The Oxford Dictionary of the Christian Church.* 2nd edition, Oxford: Oxford University Press, 1974.

Deen, Edith, *All of the Women of the Bible.* New York: Harper and Row, 1955.

Fuller, Reginald H., *A Critical Introduction to the New Testament.* London: Duckworth, 1971.

Gryson, Roger, *The Ministry of Women in the Early Church.* Collegeville, Minn.: The Liturgical Press, 1976.

Irvin, Dorothy, "Archaeology Supports Women's Ordination." *The Witness* Vol.63, no. 2: p. 5.

Jungmann, Josef A. *The Early Liturgy.* Notre Dame, Ind.: University of Notre Dame Press, 1959.

Kittel, Gerhard, ed., *Theological Dictionary of the New Testament.* Vol. 1. Grand Rapids, Mich.: Wm. B. Eerdmans Publishing Co., 1972.

Meeks, Wayne A., Ed., *The Writings of St. Paul.* New York: W.W. Norton & Co., 1972.

Morris, Joan, *The Lady Was a Bishop.* New York: The Macmillan Co., 1973.

The Oxford Annotated Bible (RSV). New York: Oxford University Press, 1973.

Page, T.E. and Rouse, W.H.D., eds., *The Apostolic Fathers,* Vol. 1. London: William Heinemann, 1912.

Pagels, Elaine, *The Gnostic Gospels.* New York: Random House, 1979.

_____, "Paul and Women: A Response to Recent Discussion." *Journal of the American Academy of Religion, XLII.* (1974): p. 544.

———, "Gnostic Texts Revive Ancient Controversies." *The Center Magazine*. (September/October, 1980): p. 56-58.

Perrin, Norman, *The New Testament: An Introduction*. New York: Harcourt Brace Jovanovich, 1974.

Richardson, Cyril C., ed., *Early Christian Fathers*. The Macmillan Company, 1970.

Ruether, Rosemary, "Why Males Fear Women Priests." *The Witness*. Vol. 63, no. 7, July, 1980.

———, "Mary – The Feminine Face of the Church." *Enquiry*, Vol. 9, no. 2, December, 1976 – February, 1977.

Stagg, Evelyn and Frank Stagg, *Woman in the World of Jesus*. Philadelphia: The Westminster Press, 1978.

Stanton, Elizabeth Cady, ed., *The Woman's Bible*. Seattle, Wash.: Seattle Coalition Task Force on Women and Religion, 1974.

Stone, Merlin, *When God Was a Woman*. New York: Harcourt Brace Jovanovich, 1976.

Swidler, Leonard, *Biblical Affirmations of Woman*. Philadephia: The Westminster Press, 1979.

Tetlow, Elisabeth M., *Women and Ministry in the New Testament*. New York: Paulist Press, 1980.

Von Rad, Gerhard, *Genesis*. The Westminster Press, 1978.

Whiteley, D.E.H., *The Theology of St. Paul*. Philadelphia: Fortress Press, 1972.